STANDING

NAKED

IN FRONT

OF YOU

To order additional copies of this book, contact
Toll Free 800 101 2657 (Singapore)
Toll Free 1 800 81 7340 (Malaysia)
orders.singapore@partridgepublishing.com

www.partridgepublishing.com/singapore

STANDING
NAKED
IN FRONT
OF YOU

Syv Bruzeau

PARTRIDGE

**Welcome to
Sickness
Land!**

A paradise of pain,
loneliness and reclusion,
a hell of new life-dying.

Fear not!
Entertainment awaits you;
twists and turns,
in all forms and manners.

So sit back,
Relax,
And enjoy the ride.

(Good luck)

Laugh at death,
my love,
laugh at death.
Laugh at Life
and its tricks.
Laugh, my love,
laugh, and
laugh at yourself

I watch myself.

I watch myself dying.

Funny, isn't it.
It sounds dramatic
to write this,
but it is a simple truth.

The Life force within
is getting
weaker and weaker.
Sucked out.
Drained.
I can't feel it anymore.

No more life inside.

My body feels
dead inside.
No more life.
Only pain and disease.

My body is getting
weaker and weaker.
Falling apart.

I watch myself dying.
What a weird occupation.

Cancer

is not an alien substance coming from the outside.

Cancer is my own cells that got sick.
Cancer is my own body killing itself.

The burden of stress and traumas, the strain of questions, unresolved and buried issues, reasons i have yet to discover-

       transforming into a physical reality.

The burden of past lives, present life, unnecessary memories that have been kept in anyway-

       becoming matter, sick matter.

Layers and layers of unbalanced energies that I haven't integrated or accepted-
Transgenealogic traumas that I carry, the long line of maternal side affecting me-

       metamorphosing into disease.

Emotions, family and society believes-

       altering the nature of my cells.

Without me realising.

Starting so long ago.
A time long enough for disease to take form, mature, and multiplicate.

It is actually a wonder,
that I am still alive,
or that the cancer
had not fully manifested
earlier.

I am killing myself.
The process has started.

In the past, I have already wished to die, to kill myself.
Today, it is taking an unexpected form.

Cancer,
are you
another kind of **suicide**?

Cancer

I am getting to know you more and more
as you speak louder and louder.
You have already
been with me for a while.

Is it our final dance?

Cancer

You are the outcry of my body
or my soul trying to reach out.
Trying to tell me something.

It is about time I listen to you.

I must look at this new reality,
and try to find answers and reasons.

I cannot silence you with medicine, hospital, doctors.

As much as possible, I must allow you,
to be raw.

For me to dive deeply into it.

       There is no other way.

       You and me.
       On our own.

    ~~~~

Body, oh my body, I am listening.
I feel you through the pain you give me.

Stomach, solar plexus, oesophagus, throat,
the whole digestive area,
the whole front part of my body
is so painful.

Burning. Screaming.

I can't even bear the touch of my tee-shirt.
Even breathing becomes painful.
It burns.

I can't bear my breath.

I feel nauseous most of the time.
I feel i am going to throw up anytime.
Or is it going the other way with diarrhoea ?

My body has become a nice little gamble,
who wants to bet?
"Les jeux ne sont pas faits" however, the
outcome remains unpredictable.

Either way, the scenery and the feelings are not pretty.
I would not like to be a toilet.
Such bad karma.

I'd rather be a telephone pole; or a crocodile;
even a cockroach would be fine; or a spatula;
maybe a pen?
I know! being a dragon would be awesome!

Ohhhh, I am throwing up.....

Body, my new reality.
I am listening.

~~~~

I have the capacity to heal my body.

Do I want to heal?

When does one know, it is time to die?
Time to stop fighting for life,
and to accept death?

What is called "**Surrender**"?

what is called "**Giving up**"?

Dying...

Death
has been romanticized, sweetened,
idealized, glorified.

But no such sweet writing about dying.

Dying is not cool,
neither sweet nor beautiful,
definitely not romantic.

Dying is painful,
ugly
humbling
lonely.

Dying doesn't offer any special VIP treatment.

It brutally brings me back to my human condition
of bones, flesh, blood, vomit.

Dying is embarrassing, even awkward.
For the dying and for the people around.

What to do?
How to behave?
Where are the instructions?

Dying is lonely.

Very lonely indeed.
People around cannot share my dying and my
experience.
And I cannot share with them either,
this deeply, intimate experience.

The dying should suffer in silence, in the corner
of dark corridors.
Sshhh, do not disturb the happy whirlwind of the
world .
Do not question the quest for eternal youth
and beauty with your dying grin and smell.

Dying

a unique experience

watching, feeling
the decay of the body
the cracking of the bones
being eaten alive

Death would actually be a relief
                    a saviour
from the awfully human process
of dying....

                        oh, the sweetness of dying
            which makes life so much tastier...
                    ~~~~

Trees,
Thank you.
Thank you for being here.

~~~~

Interesting how much Humans fight for Life, strive for
it, even if life eventually comes down only to suffering.
I guess as long as there is life, there is still hope. And
Humans can't live without hope.

Humans are afraid of not knowing.
They are afraid
of the ending.
of what lies after.
of not controlling anymore.
of not deciding.

Dying is the first taste of all this.
Death is the final kiss.

Death reminds us, of our condition,
our finitude,
our limitations.

Death puts us back into our reality,
the reality of nothingness,
of being nothing, in relation to the Universe;
of being limited.
And not invincible either.

Death also talks to our fascination
for the mystery beyond,
for violence and misery,
for destruction.

Between terror and fascination,
we live.

Strange, isn't it.

                    ~~~~

Cancer

Are you the only one who has invaded
my body?

What about **this pain**
I deal with
all the time:
Who are you?

bONES, PaiNFUL

Inside my elbows, arms, legs, top of the feet
and hands, hips, sitting bones, spine.
I can't rest my arms or elbows on a table, lay
on the floor, sit on a chair, have two bones
touching each other,
because it is too aching.

The mere existence of my bones gives me so
much pain.

It feels like some drilling into my bones.
Or an iron grater grating other bones.
Or iron claws digging deep into my bones,
Or as if my bones were madly squeezed,
and crushed.

It all started a year ago,
with some crackings in my legs bones.
Then the sensation of bones falling apart
started.
Now this drilling-grating-digging.

pAIN iN mY LEGS

Like waves of shivers.
Or being eaten up. by what?
Or filled with cement.
No life inside anymore.
My legs, my bones, stopped breathing.

bODY, faLLING APArT

Very often I feel like my body could collapse
anytime.
The only way to keep my whole body together,
to prevent it from being scattered right here,
right now,
is to tense it,
to keep all the different parts together very
mindfully.

I need to carefully and constantly keep it tight
to make sure it stays together.
It is exhausting.

pAIN iN mUSCLES.
pAIN IN NErVEs

As if someone is madly pulling my muscles
in opposite directions... to the extreme.
To rip them off?

And my nerves, oh my nerves.
So much pain inside of them,
they too, feel like they are being stretched
and stretched.

Some days, I really want to take a knife ,
cut my nerves open, take them out,
to be free of them.
Or see what is there.

sHIVERS

My body is shivering from inside.
What a strange sensation.
My liquids – my blood, my energy - moving
inside
in disturbed waves.
Such a rush. Such a storm.
What is happening?

And sometimes only silence.
A dead silence.
No life there anymore.

wEAKENED BoDY

I am getting so weak.
I can't hold a book unless it is very thin and
light. Holding a cup becomes strenuous.
All those everyday objects weigh a ton now.
Even my clothes are so heavy on my body.

My body has become too heavy for itself.

rASH

On my skin. Here and there.

My skin cannot stand itself.
My skin wants to be free of itself. To get out.
I want to rip it of. My skin is screaming. I am
screaming.

My whole body cannot stand itself,
and wants to run very very far away.

How comfortable is that?
No, it's not even about comfort anymore,
because comfort does not exist anymore.
It's about how to be with the pain?

And thoughts come: aM i CRAzY?
Is it only in my mind?
Am I imagining it?
Am I crazy?

Some of the people I talked to about it,
induced that it was indeed only in my mind.
Do they know what they are talking about??

oh dear, am I crazy?!
but what does crazy mean anyway?
i don't know anymore.
I don't take any explanations or concepts for
granted.
I must find out myself.

If doctors or therapists
don't know what it is,
why don't they just admit it?
How shocking it is
to deliberately discharge oneself
of a responsibility
and blame me??

I actually don't need doctors explanation
for myself.
But others (my family) certainly do.
It tires me.
This society-people way of doing
and thinking tires me.

The word pain is such
a weak and simplistic word
to describe the many sensations and happenings
in my body.

Pain has many faces,
many languages
and many meanings;
many screams, and
many hopes
and many messages.

Can I understand them all?
Can I handle them all?

Pain, what do you want to tell me?

And unbelievably as it sounds,
I know deeply that

I exactly am where I should be.

And so

All is perfect

~~~~

It feels incredibly peaceful
to know that this could be
the last few months of my life.
I get such an inner calm.
Everything is just right.
The way it should be.

The world around me tastes different;
what a great way to go back to the essence,
of what is essential, what is necessary.
And get rid of the rest.

One day at a time.

One more day, one more hour,

Let's smell its fragrance, let's touch it fully.

It is precious, yet so ephemeral, impermanent,
so very much impermanent.
How much I know and understand this concept
through my body,
which is falling apart.
So impermanent....

~~~~

A hint of artsy flavour
to stay light light light
like a rose petal in the wind
or a laughter on a fresh morning

-Pain Talk-

Not a pain
really

a sensation
foreign
running down my legs
inner shivers like a faceless waterfall
wordless sprawling twisting vines
electric sparks pretending power turned off
strange weight under my skin

Not a pain
really

coldness
fluids frozen
bones ice-cubed
inner chill
sucking the warmth out of my blood
vampire of a new world order
creeping into my legs
new texture
thermostat of coldness with no cold

Not a pain
really

a crack in my bones
the tower falling apart
bones becoming sand
blown away by the first wind
sand! how to keep walking?

Not a pain
really

jolts uncontrollable twitches
altered states

Quite a pain
actually

in my bones my legs
eaten alive
slowly
by alien angelic monsters
hundreds of vampires
clinging onto my bones
feasting on them

Quite a pain
actually

walking penguin style
Wood-like heavy yet weightless legs
hitting the pavement
strong strong resonance
to anaesthetise pain

cracks numbness coldness being eaten

A strong pain
actually

bones grated and drilled
as deep as one can go
muscles and nerves insanely stretched out
by an invisible hand
or compressed under unfathomable weight
steel-like claws digging in the flesh

no body anymore
alive pain only

One day
will come
Unbearable pain

the day when i will not be walking
anymore

La terre
est bleue
Comme
une orange

Rimbault

~ ~ ~ ~

How much pain can I stand?

just breath, little one,
breath softly.
one breath at a time.
breath softly.
one breath at a time.
breath softly,
one breath at a time.

~ ~ ~ ~

The everyday mundane actions have become
laborious. They all require negotiations now.
Negotiating my breath, negotiating my every
move in order to use the least energy, and make
these actions less painful.

It makes me acutely aware of every part of my
body. That is the positive side of being in pain!
Nerves of mine, i know now where you are,
muscles of mine, i know your beginning and end,
bones, i live with you.

But you make my everyday life so challenging.
How to carry this body?
How to talk and breath?

It all requires so much energy.
Energy I don't have anymore

~ ~ ~ ~

Spine, spine, spine
you hurt.
Ooohhh you hurt.
Nails all along my spine.
Permanent crucifixion.

Seriously, who is afraid of
acupuncture??
They should meet my spine
and its nails
ah ah!

~ ~ ~ ~

I

GOT

SICK

IN ORDER TO

REMEMBER

I am going through some real unusual and
strange experiences lately.

Some times it feels as if my body does
not exist anymore;
I bump into people, into windows,
into anything that comes in my way.
I can't evaluate anymore,
the physical space my body takes.
Some part of me truly believes I can get under
a door, through a wall or a keyhole.
Because i don't think of myself as a body
anymore.
I forget I have a body.

Distorted space.
Absence of space.
Absence of body.
I am no body.
I am no more.

I fall into others' identity.
I identify myself with people around,
becoming them for a second.
I look around, and suddenly I become that guy
crossing the road and I cross the road for him.
I look at a woman wearing super high heels and
wonder how I can walk and why on earth I
bought those shoes.
And I start walking very carefully so that I don't
twist my ankles.
What about that man texting while walking and
suddenly I become extremely careful because I
really need to watch my steps while texting.
Or i am that tree, over there.

Strange. Very disturbing.
I am not me anymore.
I am no one.
I am everyone.

What is this "I" anyway?
What is it that still exists?
this "I" is nothing
but an aspect of the whole,
like a costume of some sort.
It definitely is not what matters.
Hence it becomes
interchangeable.

I also receive some memories from...
other lives(?)
passing through me as I walk.
I feel voices and presence, shivers, goose-bumps,
cold showers from the top of my head.
I see people and places from other lives
(mine? others'?) while walking down the streets.
I hear noise, languages and stories from long
ago.

I am here.
And there.
I am nowhere.
I am everywhere at once.

It is actually pretty cool.
My little mind gets scared of course
because these experiences
go far beyond the scope of its understanding.
But if i remove the mind
and its labels,
I touch a truth.

~~~~

Life is just like going from one room to another.

From one life to another.

From one world to another realm.

~~~~

people accept - or are curious about -
next life,
next journey.

but they don't accept death.

~~~~

slowing down
no other choice

time stretches or shrinks
- i don't know anymore

only the **NOW** matters
no choice either

~~~~

I have no where to go
I have no home

Investigating through dance, the pain in my spine.

Snake-like rope tying me to my ancestors,
who were never given the chance to live fully,
and to express themselves.
They are only shadows.

Shadows of ashes. Empty forms.
They wait for me to save them from
this latent situation where they are trapped.

The rope goes deep,
far into many lives, many ancestors.
Where is the end of it?
I don't know.

Shadows of ashes. So many of them.
Looking at me.
Waiting.
Expecting me to set them free.
Commanding me to do so.

All their regrets, fears, aborted hopes,
anger, wars, loss, sadness
growing insanely inside my spine.
Hurting.

Grandma, are you among them?

~~~~

This is the end of a cycle for me.

A cycle during which I have to learn human
sufferings, human condition,
both in its most beautiful and painful sides.

Learn not merely intellectually,
but most importantly experientially,
physically, in my own body and flesh.

To grow.

Is my core to somehow heal others?
I will heal them better if I know suffering.

                                    If I survive, that is.

                          ~~~~

I cannot dance anymore.
I cannot perform.

My body is getting too painful
and too weak.

And besides dancing would not reflect
what I feel now,
what I go through, who I am,
and who I am not.

Because in front of the audience,
I would have to do a very soft version
- in order not to scare them.

Are you afraid of a dying Butoh dancer?

I am not able to dance anymore.
I am a dancer. I cannot dance.
Who am i?

At times I feel I became just a number,
a case, a $$ amount,
for some of the healing world and
their practitioners
(fortunately not all of them).

Welcome to another realm.
A circus of a kind.

                          ~~~~

"The pain of being Human
says Eugene Kennedy

"...There is a kind of pain in life that has nothing
to do with sickness.
It is the suffering of healthy people, as
undramatic as it is inevitable, as commonplace
as it is uncomforted.

It is the pain with a thousand private faces, the
pain that comes from being human.

Such everyday suffering deepens and changes but
never really lessens.

And the worst thing about the pain of being a
human is that it doesn't kill us.
/so true/

The pain of being alive,
the pain of always having to face challenges,
the pain of wanting love,
and the pain of finding it,
the pain of starting again, when we don't feel
like it."

                          ~~~~

                          good morning sun
                          hello birds
                          hello my breath

                          i love you

                          yeh yeah yeah,
                          darling pain,
                          i love you too

                          ~~~~

i am tired.
i am so tired.

Smile, little one, keep smiling.

~~~~

"...You give up too much of life when you try to eliminate hurt from your experience. "

~~~~

The sadness of death is experienced by the livings.
Not by the dying.

This thought has kept me going on and on in the darkest hours in the past. It has kept me alive.
Thinking of my family, and of their sadness if i was dead.

Damn, damn family.

Now is the time to think of myself first.

Yet, how to do these things right?
The point is not to hurt them.
The point is to die.

~~~~

Love is powerful

But not destructive

'**My**' cancer?
like 'my' socks or 'my' book?

it is not 'my' cancer.
it is a cancer.

some people seem to develop an attachment to
their disease.
funny.
another way to be defined, to get an identity,
or a role in this society.
they appropriate their disease and cling to it.
it is probably reassuring to them.
they know where they stand.

~~~~

There is a frog in Alaska which goes so far
as to freeze solid in a block of ice in winter time, thawing
out and coming back to life again in the spring.
How cool is that!

~~~~

What makes a gene good at surviving?
It helps other genes to build bodies
that are good at reproducing and surviving,
bodies that live
long enough to pass on the genes,
that helped them to survive.

Isn't it interesting to notice that genes,
in order to survive,
need to **help** others,
not attack or kill each other.

Wouldn't it be amazing, world-transformative,
if it was the same with Humans?!

~~~~

In the James Bond movie "Skyfall", the villain
asks 007:
"-Everyone has a hobby. What's yours?
-Resurrection."

That is exactly how I feel today:
resurrected!

Feeling a bit better today.
Yesterday I felt so shitty, that I am amazed
this morning at the joy, peace and wonder of a
life with less pain.

I am amazed at the deep feeling of calm in body
and heart,
just like after a storm.

I am so grateful for it.
It will not last.
I savour it.

Life is fantastic, despite pain and sickness.

People!
You are lucky to be healthy, to suffer no physical
pain.
Enjoy, enjoy this state of pain-free world.

~~~~

There are NO normal circumstances anymore.
No more normal physical conditions.
No more normal situations.
No normal thoughts.
No normal way of living.
No more normal goals, or wishes for the future.

It is now the 'abnormal' circumstance of
being sick.

Welcome to the world of sickness.
Welcome to Cancerland!

~~~~

...Death might not be the one
knocking at my door.

Life might be first.

I am watching
Rain falling

Low grey sky;
Thunder fantastically loud -
Lightning.

The world is grey and rainy.

I love it.

Rain and grey are **home**.

I find peace and comfort in this weather,
It is soothing to my senses.

One colour – grey
One taste – water rain
One sound - rain
One smell - rain
One touch – rain drops

This unicity is so calming.

I don't know why this weather feels like home
for me.
I trace it back to the first days of the universe,
when everything was water, everything was sort
of unicolour – brownish grey or greyish brown -
everything was simple.
Only one thing was needed: breathing.
Expanding and shrinking in order to survive.
Expanding and shrinking, in total harmony with
the surrounding.

Everything was in perpetual movement at that
time, ever so subtle, that it was hardly
perceivable.
Expanding and shrinking with the breath,
with the movement of the breath.

I was **amoeba**

a single-cell creature lying in half water.
Expanding and shrinking with the breath,
with the water.

I was in the water.
I was water.

It was home.

I have such a vivid picture and feeling of that
time...

Continuous perpetual movement
Continuous perpetual breath
Continuous perpetual transformation
and adaptation
Every second or every thousand years
Time had another dimension

Transforming
Adapting
To survive

Breathing
in the rain
in the water
in one color
in silence

It was breathing home

All we had to do was
breath
listen
breath
listen

A wonderful solitary world
Where everything was however, so dependent
with all the other breaths.
Genesis by the millions,
birthing with each breath,
in the water.

I was amoeba breathing,
lying in half water,
in a grey silent world.
Expanding and shrinking.
Always the same, always different.

Humble amoeba
Breathing the birth of All.
Sacred permutations.
Assembled membranes and breaths.
Intimately involved.
Yet so solitary.

~~~~

So, if I am killing myself,
I can also heal myself.
These two extreme opposites are equally true.

I am **A SCAVENGER** and **A SAVIOUR**
at the same time

My own **KILLER**,
and **HEALER** together

I have to admit, that the thought of my own cells
killing my body is rather disturbing.
But hey, am I surprised?
Not a bit.
I have always been pulled towards auto-
destruction.
So here we are, Darling.

And now?
Shall I try experimenting with healing myself
through
every thought,
every action I take,
every move,
every food I eat,
every emotion?

Through every energy I refuse to keep, if it
doesn't serve me right?

Through every past that I must dig out and let go
of?
Through everything I carry around, or rather in,
for others that I must recognise and unladen?

I shall become an archeologist

Digging layers and layers
of energetic sediments.
Dusting off what is not necessary anymore.
Cleansing, accepting, acknowledging;
in order to reach the core, to make it entirely
visible.
Make it shine again;
cleaned off thousands of clusters.

My body and my mind shall turn into a huge
excavating site,
an endless unfinishable work in process.

.... or shall I turn my back to healing
and call death forward?

~~~~

It is lonely today...

I want to die.
Being dead
is simpler.

We spend so much time, money and effort
learning skills for a job, a hobby or pleasure.
Yet we do not invest on happiness.
We do not work on it, learn or study it.
We let ourselves starve.

It should be our Number one priority,
since everything derives from happiness.
But it isn't.
How so??

Aren't we strange creatures?

It is easy to see Life as harsh.
It is hard to see it lightly, and be light.
It is easier to disdain than to embrace.
It is easy to be critical or sarcastic. Judgmental.

Why?
Shouldn't it be the opposite?

Is it because those attitudes give us a feeling of
power, intelligence, knowledge, sophistication?

Strange creatures we are indeed.

Being positive and happy requires modesty,
humility, courage, a sort of innocence and
wonder. Qualities not so much in fashion
nowadays.

We might be laughed at, rejected, perceived as
a dummy, or an uninteresting, insignificant
character to cast aside.

What is there to say when you are happy and
have nothing to complain about, to nag at, to
criticize?

On the contrary, you can endlessly talk about
unhappiness. Even brag about it.

Our society (or our human trait?) dictates that it
is cool to be unhappy.

We feel 'special', being unhappy.

Ahh, the battles of the ego;
to win the supremacy of attention, even if it
does, insanely, include fighting for the biggest
unhappiness.

Strange creatures we are....

We admire unhappiness, dramas, disasters.
They become the new gods.
So much fun, excitement, thrill, dread,
to talk about unhappiness.

Happiness on the other hand is boring, dull,
outdated.

Yet, as soon as unhappiness really strikes home,
we become the least courageous lambs, moaning
and coveting.

Unhappiness is cool only to talk about.
When it happens in others' life.
Or when we pretend to be so unhappy and cry on
our fate.

But when it comes a little too close,
too real,
no, thank you very much.

What is this fascination for unhappiness,
for darkness, this inclination for its shadow?

Strange, strange creatures we are.

And if we are inherently good,
something must have gone terribly wrong
since we were born,
looking at the state of the world,
and people's attitudes.

It might be correct to assume that
we are innately bad?

~~~~

All right, i declare this week
the week of the lists.
Ready? Go :

I am happy when
I make others happy
I am happy when
I am goofy
I am happy when
I am in Nature
I am happy when
I read
I am happy when
get lighter
I am happy when
I take the time to do and appreciate
all the small things in life
I am happy when
I laugh
I am happy when
I am aware
I am happy when
I eat tofu
I am happy when
I achieve something,
when i go successfully beyond my limits
I am happy when
I speak foreign languages
I am happy when
i dance butoh
I am happy when
I travel - even if i don't move
I am happy when
I create with my hands
I am happy when
I am in silence

My little happiness involves others

My little happiness induces humour to stay light,
fresh in the reality of things

My little happiness needs simplicity,
a constant rid of what's not necessary
(stuff, people, thoughts, relationships, food)

My little happiness includes awareness,
creativity, achievement -however small it might
be- challenge, and expansion of the definition,
and vision of self

My little happiness involves awe in front of the
indescribable = Nature = mystery of Life

My little happiness involves silence and beauty

My prime recipes for happiness

-Follow my passion or my instinct
(even if it makes sense only to me)
-Stay away from negative people
-Always go back to my essence -orhowtocallit?-
and take decision from that place
-NOW, be in the now
-Nobody else can decide for me
-Act the way I want to feel
-I do not need to please everyone
-Be gracious
-Allow others to help me, it is a gift from them
to me
-Keep it simple, oh yeah i love this one!
-Make everyone feel special, because they are
special
-Aim high
-Do not be afraid/ashamed to fail.
People actually do not really notice much my
failures or mistakes. I am the only one who does.
And I am the only one who gives myself pressure
to 'succeed'

And my little recipes that change my little life

-Smiling always makes things work
-Laughter often softens a situation
-Take the time
-Tofu is always best
-Less always better than more
-Cheaper is not necessarily the right answer
-A small surprise/gift to others once in a while
-Do not expect any credit from others, or them
to be grateful. Do whatever I need for myself,
for my own growth

Done.

I am very happy now.
I am sick and in much pain.
But I could not be happier.

I AM HAPPY

CHOOSING MY LIFE

AGAIN AND AGAIN

BEING IN ALIGNMENT

LIVING THE BEST VISION OF MY SOUL

as much as possible,
when the little mind
does not get too much
in the way, ah ah

.

... though I have been
DEEPLY UNHAPPY as well.
Or desperate.

But that's another chapter...

~~~~

Does my death have a purpose?
i wonder.

How to give it a purpose, a meaning?
How to have it serve others?
How to turn it into an inspiring learning
experience for others?

How could my death be a message of
growth, hope and life-embracing;
instead of guilt, fear, remorse, over-grief for
others, especially for my family?

Is it necessary?

It is not the length of a life that matters,
it is its intensity.

Remember Little one, Little Syv
Remind them,
my family, friends, people.

And remind them that they are
not responsible for me,
for my choice, for my life,
and for my death,
for how I choose
to manifest both...

~~~~

Waking up feeling down in spirit and body.
I want to curl into a little ball,
and wait for better days to come.

The loneliness of being sick...

Some days I wish I could die fast,
and with less pain.

How much longer
do I have here,
on earth?
When will I die?

~~~~

Inside Out
How my body
looks like

Mutating body

Bones growing wildly
Out of shapes
Out of my space
Out of proportion

Body killing itself

Rejecting life
Factoring bombs
Creating intricate subtle havoc
Carving unholy holes

A tree I am
An unknown creature

Nature turning mad
Forgetting the path

Eating in eating in
Eaten alive eaten alive
Who is the outside
Who, the inner world

Whose voice do you speak
Loud and louder
The sick screams
Matter becomes
To prove the
Physicality
Of mind
Of unheard
Past
Memories
Darkness

Whose voice do you speak
My own
I don't recognise
Voice like a
Stranger
A cloth
I put on
A land I
Forgot to
Explore
Too far away
Lost the key
Traces of
Ashes
Blown by
Blood
A taste of
Otherness
Sticking to my skin

Who are you
Voice screams madness
Of the disease

I can handle pain so far.
I can handle loneliness so far.
It is harder to handle the waves of sadness
when they come.

They are a full-powered tsunami taking over my
mind and gripping my solar plexus.

It is hard to stay equanimous, and not be
overwhelmed.

They come unexpectedly.
What triggers them?
Where do they come from?
Who are they?

Some is my own sadness.
Some is not.

Is it mainly the sadness of my helplessness?
I look around at people, at myself.
I feel lots of compassion and immense sadness.

Is it depression?
This feeling of sadness turns me outward,
toward my ancestors, others,
my self as part of the whole.
While depression usually turns inward,
I cannot think or care for others when I am
depressed...

Sadness,
Who are you?

In those times when sadness fills my body
and spirit,
I have not found, yet, a way to deal with it.
I feel powerless, unable to wish for life, to wish
for anything anymore.

Sadness,
more than cancer,
you are
my most elusive
and deadly mystery.

Sadness,
can we be friends?

~~~~

The necessity to think and feel my body,
in a new way.
The necessity to move my body,
in a new way.
The necessity to acknowledge my body,
in a new way.
The necessity to talk to my body,
in a new way.

My body is not one obedient piece.
It is rather, a multitude
of separate parts
living
different lives,
all having
a different agenda,
speaking various languages.
And in this cacophony of pain
they all try to reach out to me

~~~~

I create bubbles,

flowers,

memories of happiness,

laughter,

joy,

peace,

contentment

For the blue, low days.

~~~~

I am losing my mind

An awful and dreadful feeling.
It lasted only shortly I think,
but it was so terrible.

The inability
to feel my body physically and consciously

The inability
to know whether I had clothes on, or was
naked

The inability
to remember who i was, where i was,
and why i was here

It freaked me out.

I don't mind
(ah ah, what an expression, indeed,
no mind anymore)
the pain, the fucking cancer,
and whatever is eating me from the inside.
I don't mind the loneliness of being sick.
I don't mind not being able to dance because
my bonespinemusclesnerves hurt.
I don't even mind the waves of sadness.

But I DO MIND my sanity.

One more step,
one more depth,
in the experiential knowledge
of being a human being?

There is worse than physical pain caused by a
disease:

Losing one's mind

I guess I thought I would be very old if this
would happen to me.
Like Alzheimer.

You know, something for old people.
I am not old yet.

I would rather not have experienced that, if my
opinion were asked.
Hey, can i have a saying in the way i am falling
apart?
Obviously not.

How do I **surrender** to **losing my mind** ?!

Friends, enjoy, enjoy, enjoy
your full state of mind.
Oh please.
You never know when it is going to betray you...

Here I am, crying my heart out,
because I am afraid.
I am losing my mind.
I am scared. I am alone.
I don't know what happens.
I don't know what it means.
The little mind is the loudest one between us
right now.
I cannot listen to the voice of my soul to find
explanations
- or to go away from explanations.

right now i don't care.

i am just scared.

~~~~

i am listening

listening

listening to you

STOP LIVING

in the

CHAOS

My life has often been chaotic,

an open question,

no answer to how/where/what.

Pretty great life

it has been in a way.

Maybe not so peaceful,

I come to realise.

I live in the chaos.

The chaos is killing me now.

I am killing myself, by staying in the chaos.

~~~~

I am not your intellectual experiment
on death and living
I am not a concept
I am not a movie
I am not a book on death
I am not a case

I am Syv

A human being
A girl
With emotions, feelings, dreams.
Still alive

~~~~

Where

and What

is my refuge?

The 'innocent' question turned into a dreadful
or an awkward second of eternity (for me):

"How are you?"

How do I answer?

Take the polite white lie option, easy, expected,
of "I am fine".
No questions asked or wanted, no answers
expected.
Take the brilliant unnerving American way "I am
great" with the most glowing, lying smile?
Take the middle way of a smile only?
Take the humourous way of "My cancer is fine
today, thank you very much" or
"I am going to vomit on your shoes right now"?
Or shall I launch myself into the description of
the various pains and discomfort?

It sounds like a simple question. Yet...

And how to deal with the solicitude of those few
who know and care, and who truly wait for an
answer?

How to deal with the so-far-unresolved balance
between what is to be said, or not (said)?

Ahh, being sick is quite a full-time job in dealing
with others and oneself.

Just smile, Little one, Little Sunshine,
stay quiet and smile...

~~~~

Better keep my condition to, and for myself.
is the best way I find to deal with it.

Fewer questions and answers. Stay anonymous.

No endless advice to hear (I know they come
from the heart, but I don't always want to hear
about what I should/should not/must/must not
do, and about infinite miracle potions...)
No temptation to become a 'poor little me', a
suffering victim, and miss the opportunity for
growth.

Not everyone wants to hear the ugly truth of life
coming to an end. Not everyone wants to be
reminded of their own death and mortality,
through my sickness and pain.

Ahh, dying as a hero, yes! Anytime.
Dying of a sudden painless death, anytime.
Dying slowly in pain, no no no no no.

~~~~

If my bones and my muscles fall apart,
will my skin and my breath be strong enough to
support my body, to make it stand and walk?
I wonder.

If I hang my skin with clothespins to the sky,
to the clouds, to the air,
will I be all right?
Little silly me. Proud to be.
The day I am not silly anymore,
my soul is dead.

~~~~

I look around and see so much misery.

Misery in the heart, in the spirit, in the mind,
in the body, in the future.
I feel so much compassion for human beings.

So much misery and fear which should be
replaced by acceptance, joy, awareness.

It is not easy to be a Human Being

~~~~

Do not be afraid, people.

As long as you are healthy in your body and your
mind (and even if you are not healthy),
there is nothing to be afraid of.
The stress, questions, issues of the everyday life
are just a disturbance.

Trust me.

I know you cannot fully understand it.
But trust me.
And do not wait to understand it.
Do not be afraid, now.

~~~~

~~Pure Raw Pain~~
~~today~~
~~No more ego~~
~~no more mind~~
~~no more heart~~
~~No more i~~
~~only~~ *~~Pure Raw Pain~~*

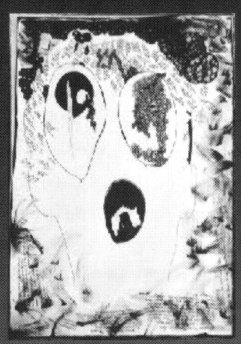

My face not mine anymore.
My face became pain.

Pain, a traveller in bodyspace

And I shall

love my cancer cells

For they are
the lonely ones -
the ones
who have been abandoned

For they are
part of me -
they are me

For they are
the ones who need most love -
and support

I shall

forgive my cancer cells

Forgive myself,
for ending up here

Forgive myself
for having been careless,
blind, weak

Forgive myself
for the pain that is to come

Can I truly forgive myself?

~~~~

to Disappear...

DO NOT BE AFRAID

OF

YOUR

IMMENSITY

Go against beliefs,
against society,
against what is,

and die.

Even if it sounds like
a suicide
of some sorts.

Follow my instinct,
on the knowledge that
my life is done,
and it is all right to move on
to the next level/life/whatever
will be,
which is a feeling
I have been having
for so long.

If this is what I feel inside,
why not?
But is it,
truly ?

Go beyond the idea
of how the world
is supposed to work;
how we are supposed to act,
or react.

Go beyond concepts.
A major one being
"Life is precious".
yes it is ...but

Why not recognize it,
when it is time
to go.

Why not have the right
to decide to go.
It would make life
even more precious,
would not it?

Animals commit suicide
when it is their time to die,
or to preserve their species.

Why not us,
why not me?

How can I know for sure?

It might sound like nonsense,
and I can't properly explain
what my sub-consciousness feels,
I can't quite put the finger
on the exact spot;
but it is something along this line:

Knowledge, concepts,
and the world as we know it,
are shifting,
and we have to shift with it.
Embrace the shifts,
even if I don't totally understand them,
whether they are pure madness,
or the future Truth
— or new awareness.

Touching some reality that is still unknown.
Reality which might oppose
my certainty,
my beliefs,
my way of thinking.

It is challenging
Destabilising.

Because I can't explain to others what this is,
hence I'm having a hard time justifying
the path I might take.

This is how it feels to step out of
the safety
of my own prison,
my cage of certainty.

To open myself
to the vast understanding of the Universe;
energies, powers.
And connect to my soul.

All different,
from our habit of mind
in our humanness.

We should have the right to leave.

By dying,
I am merely transitioning
to my next experience.

How can I explain that
to my family and my friends?

Suicide is the killing of the body.
The body only.

Why not it being the way
to set the soul, the self,
free to go to the next experience?
Like Sallekhana

~~~~

DANCING MY CANCER

Cancer trapped
in the limit of my body,
in my skin.

How to get out of this body?

How to move, live, spread?
How to feed on other healthy cells?

Dancing it

                    Cancer exists with what I gave it,
                    and still am giving it, to live on.

        I am the feeder, and the one being eaten alive.

Dancing it

                Do my cancer cells want what I give them?
                    Would they rather be healthy?

We have big mouths and devour the other cells.
We are endlessly hungry.

              Do they know otherwise, another way perhaps?

           Death is not an alien creature which has invaded my body.
                Death comes from inside; from myself.
We are your death.

                Nobody is a victim of cancer.
            For how can you be a victim of yourself?

                There is no one to blame but myself.
                    But why blame myself?
                  A waste of time and energy.
            Better to forgive myself, love myself.
            Love the sick, and the healthy parts.

Dancing it all
tonight

Getting weaker and weaker.

How to shower now?
Simply standing there is draining.
I can't reach my feet anymore.
I painfully sit down in the shower and try to
clean my feet. How to stand up again? The
slippery tiles of the wall gives me nothing to
grab on to, to pull me up.

My whole body hurts.

Standing, sitting.
Such natural and easy actions I had never
thought about before, that i took for granted.
They are so painful and exhausting now.

How to put my clothes on now?
I break down every single move
into counting, and breath.

1, breath in, get ready, breath out
2, breath in, brace myself, breath out
3, breath in, one arm in my bra strap, breath
out
4, breath in, try to get the other arm in,
breath out
5, breath in, reach behind to fasten my bra,
hoping very much i can do it at once, breath
out
6, breath in, rest, breath out
7, breath in, brace myself for the tee-shirt,
breath out

and so on and so forth for the rest of my
clothes.
It is exhausting.

The thought of going out tires me so much.
So many movements are required.
Here again I break them all down into counting
and breath.

Switching the light off and opening the door
have become heroic projects.
I need to get ready for every mundane
movements, gathering will power and strength
to go through every single moment of my daily
life.

And when i reach the corner of the street,
it is a small, yet beautiful victory.

Counting in English, French, Japanese, Russian,
smile counting, silent counting, singing
counting.
I became the International Counter.

**Being a human being,
is indeed
so exhausting.**

My life is therefore very much reduced.

So many things have become unnecessary
and meaningless.
Pain has made my life boil down
to what is
absolutely necessary.

And actually,
not much
is truly necessary.

If i could go out in the streets naked,
it would simplify my life greatly.
Frankly speaking, who needs clothes?
Unless you live in a cold country,
they are not part of the survival kit.
Not mine anyway.
It would be so simple,
if I was living in the jungle
or among some tribes.
They are the smart ones.

Civilisation has made life way too complicated.

I love the ramps in Singapore.
This amazing space, tilted to perfection,
to help me go up.
I dread stairs and steps,
which are so painful for my body
and so exhausting.
One step feels as challenging as a building
to climb.
A short flight of stairs,
is my Everest.

I like the bus.
Its seats are quite soft
for my painful sitting bones.
The seats of the MRT
are on the contrary - too hard.
I wish i had the strength to carry a cushion
everywhere with me.
I don't have the strength
anymore, for that either.

i like the numerous benches available,
to rest my painful and tired body
— even if they are too hard.
The designers were obviously
not sick.

I like the escalators.
gliding up.
No steps to start the journey;
no steps to end it .
Smooth.

I like the silence.
every sound feels so loud now,
so much louder than before.
Even sounds hurt.

I like empty space devoid of people.
Agitation, movements, speed tire me.
People move too fast, too loudly,
with too many unnecessary movements
for my tired mind.

~~~~

I dread sneezing or coughing
because it sends
an awfully painful
echo
and tightening
in my spine
in my back
in my guts.

I have become much aware
of the inner connections
between the different parts
of my body.
Indeed, they are all connected.

I am a little
anatomy
and biology
class.
It is pretty chaotic
down there,
nobody is listening to the teacher.
But we learn a lot.
Hands on.

~~~~

Who wants a sick girlfriend?

Being GENTLE with myself
My full-time job now.

Taking care of myself
and
being gentle with myself
are
two different things

Allowing myself to be

soft

weak

lazy

I have never really been gentle with myself,
I think.

Time to be.

I love it.

More important than death

becoming acceptable,

Life has to become so as well.

This is probably the hardest.

Our fear of death
finds its root in
our fear of Life,
of living.

Of fully living;
aware, awake.

Of accepting who we are.
Of accepting that there is much
we don't understand.
Starting with Life itself — and its purpose.

For me at least,
accepting Life
has been the greatest challenge.

I fully lived.
I love Life - somehow - sometimes.
Yet something in me cannot accept Life.
Something in me, wants to die.

I forgot who I am.
That is why i want to die.

When there is nor 'this' neither 'that'...

I am all the feelings.
And not one overwhelms the others.
I am everyone, and everything.

I am 'emptiness'
I am empty of feelings, stories, voices;
empty of past, of future;
empty of self.

When emptiness means...
wholeness.

When fear, anger, or sometimes guilt arises,
instead of suppressing them,
feeling bad about them,
or even only observing them...

I imagine that I am a pool
                    a space —
where those emotions float.

I am just a pool for them to pass by.

And I make sure i am vast enough,
that there are no boundaries
where those emotions can bounce off,
or cling to.

I am an endless ocean

I am the Spaciousness

Spaciousness in which
there is nothing to be lost;
therefore no fear of losing.

Just the spaciousness.

I feel it.
I feel it so much.

~~~~

My body is not mine anymore today:
it belongs to sadness and loneliness.

Be my guests, you will have to share the space with the
drilling in my bones, and the avid hungry mouths, eating
up my guts.

~~~~

And if there is still a smile in my eyes, if I am
silly goofy, insane, it is to protect myself.

A survival kit to call my own:
my medicine.

~~~~

Losing my mind,
just like losing my key,
or my phone.
What an expression.
How did i lose my mind?
Did i drop it?
Did i leave it behind in a taxi?
Was it stolen?
Can i locate it in the 'lost & found' box?

Ah ah, losing my mind.
indeed.

Probably a joke of the universe.

~~~~

Being sick is like a TV show or drama:
a mixture of pathos, comedy, terror and
unexpected twists, new characters coming, and
going.

I don't look at it with too much seriousness,
or egoistic respect, otherwise, it might turn into
a boring philosophical dilemma;
or it might become too serious, dogmatic, heavy.

Me little me might puff itself up under the
spotlight.
But at the center stage, the true main actor is
sickness.
And the true main director are the reasons
behind it.

~~~~

If I have brought this illness
on myself
because
I beautifully lived,
felt,
questioned,
with rage or hopelessness,
and fought for coming to life
despite the odds,

                              as he wrote then,

I should love my illness.

Illness which gives
a new texture, taste, direction to this life:
a new stream of thoughts.

Yes, at my own minute level, I have had such a
great life.
I've loved it.

              the good, the bad, the worst

I have been the sculptor of my own life.

I am, still, in my illness, the sculptor of my life.

Yes, I brought it all upon myself
to learn
to be more deeply
in my true nature
to understand more.

I am grateful.

                              Despite the days
                                 when I feel
                                     weary
                              of you, pain

              ~~~~

                              BabyBlue
                              BabySyv
                              Nothing matters
                              Nothing lasts

              ~~~~

Anatole Broyard says

"...to look upon the ruin of (a patient's) body as
tourists look upon the great ruins of antiquity."

Grand DECADENCE

=

GRAND LIFE!

              If the outcome is sickness,
                   I'll take it all.

Illness is a great liberator from unnecessary
layers and burdens;
"from being politically correct, to boringly
(dis)honest."

It is fantastic, given permission to be myself,
to be crazy,
wild,
straightforward,
madly honest,
silent,
goofy,
lonely,
buoyant.

When one is critically ill,
one has the right to it all.
I don't need to hold back.
I can let it all out.

Tremendous FREEDOM!

I am so lucky.
I declare illness the new chic.
An illness, anyone?

              ~~~~

好 无

魂 有

BEYOND

BEAUTY

AND UGLINESS

Who do I need to forgive?

Whom should I ask for forgiveness?

Who should I thank?

What Is Unborn In Me?
What Has Not Yet Fully See The Light In Me?

What Is It Within Myself I Don't Wish To
Experience?

I can't
expect others
to be where I am —
much less understand it.

I have to
understand
their place, their lives
their concerns, their stress.
That, is the job of the sick.

That is the only way to keep a bond with the
healthy ones:
by following their agenda.

Being closer to death doesn't bring me
superiority.
On the contrary, it should give me more
compassion,
more kindness,
and more understanding for their weakness...
and mine.

Do I sound very presumptuous?!

I am not here to give any lessons.
I am as weak and ignorant as they are.

~~~~

I hate throwing up.

The spasms of the body,
the uncontrollable clenching of my poor
stomach, when there is nothing inside but my
body still makes me throw up anyway.
The scenery of the toilet - an action movie of its
own detestable kind...
The tears,
The anger sometimes;
The exhaustion

Being sick is no fun
And not glamourous
Except in American movies...
I hate it.
I hate American movies - making it so
glamourous.

Dying, or being sick is not.
Give us a break.

~~~~

This is not

a time

for caution

Love cannot be rational

Death cannot be either

I AM THE **V**ASTNESS

.

I AM THE **S**PACIOUSNESS

.

"**I**" IS **V**ASTNESS

.

"**I**" IS **S**PACIOUSNESS

When my mind, my ego, my 'I' dissolves,
nothing else but vastness, spaciousness remains.

When, whatever "I am" means
Pure Space;
Vast Space.

Oh, this incredible,
deeply peaceful feeling
of inner spaciousness,
of inner vastness.

Where there are
no limits
no edge
no end
no limitation
no time

Infinite space only

Where the energy that I am, travels
at light speed with freedom and lightness.
Flying above this water of Spaciousness;
And being at the same time, this water of Vastness.

Where everything else that signifies life – emotions,
people, situations – do not matter anymore.

Not because I do not care, but because they become
so miniscule.
Infinitesimal spots in this Vastness, in the Vastness
that I am,
spots that will eventually go, disappear,
spots that do not impact the vastness,
spots that have nothing to feed on in this Vastness,
spots that are nothing,
in the face of this Spaciousness.

They are precious in some way,
precious in the moment they rise in the space.
They represent a precious second-long experience.

Yet they do not matter,
for they eventually vapourise:
for their fate is to vapourise.

They are equally precious,
meaningful,
and nothing.

They are the nutrition for future lives,
they are the build-up of knowledge.
Yet they are small, in relation to the Whole.
They are neither dreadful, nor worth enough to cling
to, or to be too affected by.
Even deep depression, hurts, wars and struggles,
fears are but a ripple, in this spaciousness.

Spaciousness is **who I truly am**.

Spaciousness is the **essence** of me,
and everything that is.

Spaciousness is **my core**, my home.

How do I describe in words,
what this Spaciousness is?
How do I describe with words,
what it is to BE Spaciousness ?

It is **perfection**.

It is what **is**.

It is **peace**.

It is **silence**.

Is it **pure consciousness**.

It is **pure awareness**.

Reaching from within, this Spaciousness goes far
beyond my inner being.
It encompasses the Whole, the Universe;
Everyone.
Everything is connected – my inner spaciousness,
and the Energy that exists all around,
which is 'me' too, and
who I truly am.

It is just **ONE**

One energy.

One Whole.

We are One.
No beginning. No end either.
No difference.
Nothing.
No one is more important
than another.
We all come from the same Source.
We all return to there.

I deeply, totally, feel it, live it,
taste it, know it.

So evident.

Such beauty.
Such clarity.
Such mystery.
Yet, such simplicity.

I know that in this life,
all I am doing is collecting experiences
of suffering, love, abandonment,
pain, healing.

These experiences will be transformed
into Energy;
the Energy which is everything,
and contains who I am.

Hence, I will receive knowledge
through these experiences.
I will receive the wisdom and knowledge.

And I will use them to heal,
to become a guide.

Indeed, it does not matter,
if I die soon,
it does not matter whether i die,
or stay alive.

For I am Spaciousness.
Who I truly am,
is bigger
than this illness and life.
Much bigger.

It is profound, to experience this insight.
To understand it.
Not from a book, or from a lecture.
But from my own consciousness.
My own body.
My own soul.
From a dimension
that I don't know how to call.

The direct experience
beyond life,
beyond death,
beyond ego.

This is exactly how I feel,
and what I know,
within my inner self and guts.

I know it is the truth.

It is not a kind of story I tell,
to make myself feel better.

And for now, how wonderful and peaceful
to carry this vastness within,
to be this vastness.

It makes me gently strong.

with the strength of love,
the strength of accepting the weakness,
the strength of knowing,
the strength of sacredness,
the strength of being vulnerable
and the strength to absolutely surrender.

Do not fear, dear human beings;
Do not fear.
Go and find this Spaciousness.
It is within you.
It has always been there.
It is there, waiting for you, to go back there.

Do not fear.
Come into my arms,
I will carry you.
I am strong.
I am Spaciousness
I am Love

Sorry people, sorry little mind;
I am not here to transform you.
I am here to transform myself.

I am not responsible for you.
Only for myself.

Sorry people,
I am not here to teach you anything.
I am not here to save you, or the world.
Who I am to know anyway what is best for you?

I am not even interested in leaving a mark
behind,
in making a real difference.

I am here to be myself.

Maybe I can touch someone, in some way.
Maybe I can inspire someone.
Humbly.

Maybe not.

I am here to be myself.
It is in being myself, truly, that the world can
change and be a better place.

~~~~

Are my healthy cells protesting
with disgust and rage,
at the new order in my body?

Do I give them a choice?

~~~~

my little bucket list of the day:

A comfortable bed every night
Be in Nature
Trans-Siberian trip
Creating with clay or bronze
Classical music concerts
Play in a theatre production
Learn Italian and Mandarin
Go into a submarine
Broder un habit de Lumiere
Make everyone around me happy

~~~~

I long for places of BEAUTY
For my soul

The Truth
is in
not knowing.

In the cessation
of looking for answers.

**THERE IS NOTHING,
OR NO ONE
TO BE.**

There is only

the UNNAMABLE TRUTH

of BEING

the WHOLENESS

Christmas Eve...

and it could be my last one.
a shocking realization when it really hits me,
not a mere hypothesis anymore.

which fills me with a sense of softness,
and sadness.
sadness not for myself,
but for those i will leave behind.

Today is quiet.
Only me and the birds.

Today is Christmas day.

I have books.
Clay. Writing. Being.

And I have sadness.
Pain. Uncertainty.

I have silence.
Quiet. Grey.

I have a soft, little smile
on my lips.
Very small.

I have absence.

I have cancer.
I have Death.

All is good.

I am getting so weak.
Life is leaving me.
Strength is leaving.

I need to hear from my family,
that it is ok for me to die.
I need to hear from them,
that they would let me go, when it is time.
That they will not hold on to me.

It has been a burden for so long,
the pain and guilt,
of knowing that they will not be ok,
and cannot let me go....

They need to set me free.

I understand their sadness, sorrow, anger.
But they need to work on their own emotions.
They need to look at my death
as a unique opportunity to go inward,
to touch themselves;
their truth, their peace.

Please set me free.
I know it is hard to hear, and to accept.

I need to protect no one.

Let myself die,
out of being a sister and a daughter...

I also need to give a closure.
They need a closure
to come to terms
with my potential, upcoming death;
to accept, to grieve, to be sad, to rejoice.

I will go into my Spaciousness,
and from this place of Love,
I will talk to them.

~~~~

Which emotion is more exhausting:

Grief?
Anger?
Sorrow?

~~~~

The lovely medical bills...

i have pain and some lumps in my breasts,
so I decide for once, to see a doctor.
It took a maximum of 15 minutes, and the bill
came to sg$250.

"Cash or credit card, Miss?" was the only
comment.
No way I am having the tests they suggest,
at sg$900.

I am not a cash register.
I am a human being.

The results of the test were given to me over the
phone a few days later, while I was on a MRT
subway station platform.
It was noisy around me and I could not hear
properly.

The nurse could have brought any terrible news
to me, and I would have been there, at the edge
of the platform, trying to make sense of the
phone call.

What a strange way to relate to people's health.

~~~~

two pebbles. one leaf. one breath. one butterfly.
three fingers. two cats.
thousands of clouds. thousands of pain.

~~~~

'Pain'
is a pretty gross and simplistic word
to describe
all the subtleties, and layers
that lie underneath it.

Pain
is a whole world of

textures,
sensations,
colours,
locations,
temperatures.

A universe of its own.

Inside and outside....

So, how can I limit
this multi-faceted experiencing
to one word – pain?!

Pain is still, moving, tingling.

        Drilling madly into my bones.

Compressing, flowing.

        Heavy and big, tiny bits here and there.

Under the skin or deep down.

        In my fluids or my bones.

Like a frozen lake, or fireworks.

        Thousands of needles poking my skin or
        choking my throat.

Cotton narrowing my breath.

        Pain is many rivers.

Cold like ice. Burning like fire. Or hot stones.

        Sticky. Rolling. Bubbling.

Steel hands clenching into my flesh.

        Melting. Hardening.

Grey white lava from a volcano.

        Pond of a strange liquid.

Cracks. Tensions.

        Strange silence.

Suspension of what is.

        Suspension of time.

Pain is a great teacher

How ironic,
I had been looking for
a spiritual teacher
for a while,
and I realize
I have actually
found one:

Pain.
Being sick

Through pain
I learn much about
my physical body.

And how to relate to it
About fear and resistance
About acceptance
About transcending pain
About what lies beyond

I learn to listen,
to go more and more,
into the details of pain,
of my body

Pain and being sick are my fierce teachers.

Forcing me to open,
think, investigate,
remove layers,
look at my fears and flaws in the eye.

Forcing me to realize
what life and death is
-at least try-
and perceive some truth.

Forcing me to change, surrender.

My teachers.
The teachers found the student, I guess.
Isn't it funny?

                    I am so lucky to have pain.

I am not calling for pain,
I am not a victim,
I am not passive.
I take it as it comes.

However I do not want to run away,
from the experience,
and the teachings it brings. I am not afraid of
pain.
So far.

It is the fear of pain that makes others wish,
for me not to feel pain.
Especially in our society, where pain and dying
are not socially acceptable,
and are immediately concealed,
with pain killers or all kinds of medicines and
treatments.

Fear of pain.
Most people are so imprisoned and entangled in
their fears, that they transfer it to others.

I understand their fear.
Who wants to suffer?

Yet pain is a great opportunity
to investigate,
who we are.

Of course, if the pain becomes
unbearable one day,
I don't know how I will react.
We will see.
Not to worry about it now.
One day at a time…

I am more than this physical body,
more than this limited mind.

I am not the pain,
and the pain does not define me.

~~~~

Some mornings,
when i wake up,
I am unable to move.

I know I am not paralysed,
yet I can't move my body.
Did my body forget movements?
Are the connections interrupted?

I must learn from scratch,
how to move again:

directing my intention
to a finger tip,
and slowly,
so slowly,
awakening the movement
from there.

finger tip, moving

Next finger tip.
One finger tip at a time.
The whole hand.
Then the wrist.

Hand and wrist, moving

Elbow.
Shoulder.

Slowly,
so slowly
I might be able to move
one arm.

One arm, moving

A pause.
to breath.
to gather strength.

Slowly,
so slowly,
directing my intention
to the other arm.

And so on with the whole body.

you bet,
it takes a while to get up.

What if one day
my mind is not powerful enough
to move my body?

~~~~

Sometimes I succeed
Sometimes I fail…

a day of resistance,
avoidance,
the little self taking over,
the wish to be empty,
to feel nothing,
think nothing.

I have enough

~~~~

Always remember:

THERE IS NO 'OTHER'.

It is just two perceptions,
of one existence.

There is just 'being',
experienced from different points.

~~~~

In the American Indian culture,
Life is not seen as a straight line
(where the longer the line, the more whole
we are supposed to be), but rather,
as a circle
which becomes complete at the stage of
puberty.

From that time on, one is seen as a wholeness,
that continues to expand outward.

Once the circle has formed,
anytime one dies,
one dies in wholeness.
And one can die anytime.

Wholeness is not seen as the duration
one has to live,
but as the fullness with which one enters,
in each complete moment.

~~~~

Love
is all there is

At the end of life,
when you die,
Love is all that matters.

What matters isn't your work,
or how much you have achieved
– however great and useful it could have been;
or the money you made, the titles, the study,
the knowledge you learnt,
not even how 'good' you have been,
how dutifully you meditated.

Love matters.
Only Love.

If we ever need to justify ourselves
when we die,
it will be on one thing only:

How much did we Love?
How much did we give Love?
How much did we allow ourselves
to receive Love?

Trust me, I know.
I have been there.
I died,
and I was asked

Coming to

                    emptiness

                                    about

clinging

emotions

situations

expectations

hope

disappointment

EMPTINESS...

                    ~~~~

Who is here to hold my hands,
to hug me, to tell me that I am all right??
Sometimes I need someone…

                    I am touching an edge.
                    The edge of my loneliness.

It all passes, little Syv…

                    ~~~~

Investigating my pain.

I cut my body open and looked inside:

                    I was killing myself.
                    I saw myself killing a baby,
                    who was also myself.

                              Such a shock.
                    Watching me, kill myself.

                              Oh dear, oh dear
                    So much pain and sorrow there...

                    ~~~~

And today is resurrection.
Feeling less pain.

Taking the time to sip my juice while reading the
morning newspaper.
Turning the pages. Examining the words.
Luxury. Happiness.

The 'joy' of
throwing up, nausea, diarrhoea,
weakness, pain.
The joy of
being able to stand up.

Resurrection comes and goes.

                    Today is also the LAST DAY of THE YEAR.
                    Frankly, what does it mean, 'year'?

                    ~~~~

jour de l'an
first day of the year

**The only thing I know is that
I don't know.**

I don't know
What life is
What death is
What 'I" is.

**And the truth might be in
this not knowing**

In surrendering to
this not knowing-ness

The truth is always inside of us.
We just need to remember it.

My soul, my consciousness, "I"

is not in my body.

My body is contained within my soul.

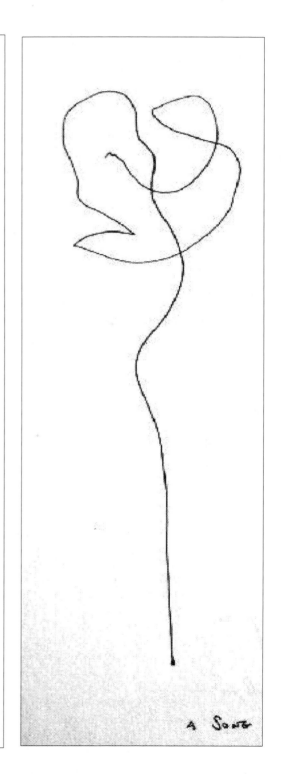

A Soné

"Sorrow prepares you for joy.
It violently sweeps everything out of your house,
so that new joy can find space to enter. It shakes
the yellow leaves from your heart so that new
green leaves can grow in their place. It pulls up
the rotten roots, so that new roots hidden
beneath have room to grow.

Whatever sorrow shakes from your heart, far
better things will take their place."

                          Rumi

                  ~~~~

We long for love, support, peace,
and when we receive it,
we don't believe it;
we don't believe it can be given to us,
that it can be genuine.

We don't believe we deserve goodness
because we don't believe in our own goodness,
in our own infinite potential...

We are always ready to live according
to our weaknesses and limitations,
and cannot believe,
that we are powerful beyond measure...

What is this insanity?
What went wrong?

Most of us want so much to be "special",
and the society in which we live now reinforces
so much this hunger, the perfect example being
facebook.
Oh, to be recognized!

But isn't our true nature
to have no specialness,
no separation,
to be one with others?

Become invisible
                  ordinary

Not in fashion these days.

We'd rather be special in our own custom-made
prison, adding a layer of false gold on the bars of
this prison, than to become free.

We are so odd. I don't get it.

                  ~~~~

My little life takes more and more
effort and time,
planning and adjusting.

I look for anything, anything at all,
to make my daily life easier,
in the way I carry and use my body,
in my choice of doing and not doing.

Reducing.
Bringing everything into a raw simplicity....

                    And the curse to be able
                      to smile and keep going,
                    that people hardly notice,
                           or don't want to,
                          because I still ....
                        because I don't ....
                            because ....
                                ....
                                 ..

                  ~~~~

I am spending most of my time on my bed now.

Except mainly to go teach butoh, putting a brave
smile on my face and on my body, and painfully
going there anyway. Such an effort. Yet such a
reward. As soon as I start guiding, pain becomes
secondary.
Only butoh remains - and the students.

My Bed - the most comfortable place in the
discomfort.
Body - not a dancing place anymore.
Only a painful one.

                  ~~~~

Cancer, i love you

i love you i love you i love you

Cancer, do not be afraid
I love you

Come, I will hold you

I will heal you

Holding my breath,
             to hold my body together —

if I breath into my body
             it is a call for decay
             and destruction

                                    A Death Chant
                            A death of my body
                            A death of my mind
                        A death of my thinking
                    A death of my movements
                            A death of the I

                                    Caressing words, I am

Healing means experiencing my true nature.

Which does not mean a cure has occured.

It only brings balance.

I don't oppose healing and dying.
Both may happen at the same time.
I might eventually heal,
yet die anyway.

I might understand and let go and remember
and forgive and make peace
and become whole.

And die anyway.

                            ~~~~

                    I am the birds, the bed I am lying in,
                        the pen, the ink, and the paper,
            thousands of senses, the glass of the window,
                        the sky, the trees, the wind,
                            the silence of my heart,
                            the pain and the peace,
            the spaciousness within, and without.

                        I am everything, everyone,
                            nothing and none.

                            ~~~~

You say I am strong.
But sometimes I am so weak alone desperate lost.
Can't you see it?

~~~~

I woke up this morning and
I wanted to commit suicide.

this was my first thought and feeling:

to
DIE

right now

Today I want a life,
with no sickness in my mind all the time.
It tires me.
To have pain always here, in my mind as well.

~~~~

I am my own lab.

I want to explore the healing part of myself,
as well as the destructive one.
I cannot explore one,
and leave the other behind.

Just like death and life are inseparable.

I cannot reflect on death,
if I don't think as well,
about what life is,
and how I live.

Rehearsing Death

Might be first

Rehearsing Living

~~~~

The Universe within my body is as vast,
as the Universe out there, outside,
and around me.
The Universe of my Spaciousness is vaster;
endlessly vaster than them all.

There is so much Love in my Spaciousness
that nothing can resist it, or bother it.

~~~~

body too weak
mind too foggy
to write

both too tired

The Roses are dead

Drilling in my bones

I was about 8-year old,
when I first
got depressed.

I felt overwhelmed by the world around me.
It looked like a black maize with rules
I didn't know about.

Nothing made sense.

I fell tremendously helpless,
in front of the unhappiness of this world.

I was desperately searching for an answer
to a question I had forgotten.

My mom's comment i learnt much later was:

> "this little one is carrying
> the sadness of the world"

Years later, today, i still am.

I DIED
the other day
lying on my bed

I know.
It is very strange, and unbelievable to say.
But it is true.
I died.

I went to another 'state',
and at the same time was so present in my body,
totally aware of what was happening.

Somehow I knew I was dying.
I was going through the process of dying.

My body suddenly became filled
with emptiness;
with silence.

My body became
Emptiness;
Silence.

Emptiness and Silence
were taking the shape of my body.
Until my body no longer existed.

My senses, one after the other, dissolved.
My body disintegrated,
into that Emptiness and Silence.

And whatever 'I" was, became
this Emptiness and Silence.

"I" was floating there,
in this great Emptiness and Silence,
and I was them too, at the same time.

I was floating between time and space.
Somewhere after not being alive anymore,
and arriving at death.

Then, "I" became everything and nothing.
I can't explain any better.
"I" became everything and nothing.

I knew I had died.
I knew for sure - although I don't know how.

There was this incredible
silence,
presence,
and energy
surrounding me;
and me,
being it all
as well

And I knew, in my deepest truth, that

There is nothing to fear
There is nothing to expect
There is nothing to build
There is no one to harm
There is nothing to cling onto

There is nothing but Love

There are no others
There is no end, no beginning
There are no boundaries

There is nothing but Love

LOVE   LOVE   LOVE

IS

EVERYTHING

And I want to tell people, again and again:

Do not fear,
Love is strong.

My love is strong,
Your love is strong.
I can take you all into my arms.
I can hold your heart and your body;
I can open the door to your soul,
who is waiting for your Love.
Listen.

You will hear it:
Love

When I got back to my bed,
I felt so detached.
Not in a bad way.
Neither a good way, actually.
A neutral one.
Detached.

When I die,
it is an out-of-body and
within-the-body experience.

When I die
it is incredible.

It is

EMPTINESS

CALM

SILENCE

WHOLENESS

So intense it has a texture.
I become it.
I find no words
to describe the texture
of these realities.
They are so vivid,
endless and timeless,
beyond human language.

When I die
there is no questioning anymore.

Because I know.
It is coming back to me.

Not in words,
but in inner knowledge.
All the wisdom and knowledge
that we have within, that we, humans,
lose on earth.

Dying is gentle.

It is a powerful,
peaceful,
a calm explosion,
to other states.

It is empowering.

Humans, do not be afraid of dying.
It is beautiful....

~~~~

Forgiveness

a powerful process,
and a release of
great energies of Love,
compassion, lightness, gratefulness.

I forgive you.

Such lightness in me now.
Such Love.

So true to say,
that not forgiving
is more destructive to the person
holding this unfinished business,
than to the one who needs to be forgiven.

Forgiveness

A sharp tightening in the chest
a tightening in the guts
Waves of resentment come rushing
engulfing every piece remaining

Revenge talks loud
Victim I certainly am
Villain, the dreadful villain he doubtless is
Ah, to despise him
To ruin him:
A goal set in the mind and the heart

Waves waves
Memories of betrayals
hurting words
Dark, unbearable silence
They feed me now
vicious, all mighty masters
of my inhuman, embittered heart

He is the one! I shout
the one responsible for my misery
For his act, he must suffer
be rejected ... no trial needed
I spit on those waves
undesirable

The lecture is ready on my lips
I am the pure innocent one
Listen to me and my misery
to my unfortunate fate
He is the blameworthy criminal

On and on and on
No end to hate
to revenge
Mocking righteousness
eating my life, from inside
My maddened head
Constant, deadly alive
weighting torment

Foggy mind becomes.
Lost in circles
on and on
Memories of betrayals
hurting words
dark, unbearable silence
dwelled upon
frantic endless outcry outcries
intoxicating every piece remaining

... ... And then
a pause ... ...

utterly unforeseeable

Serendipitously
unnoticed at first
a clearing
a lightness
a new texture in the heart
quietening every piece remaining

Listen ....

A soft lightness in the chest
a lightness in the guts
Foggy clouds clearing out
Glancing at the villain
Tenderness comes rushing
in my bruised heart
Memories betrayals
hurting words,
dark unbearable silence
still there

Yet no substance
in them anymore
no meaning
no revenge

Human i am
Human he is
No better than him
No better than me
Not more right

Waves of tenderness
understanding
come rushing
invading every piece remaining

The peaceful silence
that follows
incredibly gentle
tastes a serene exaltation

I dropped down to a new space
of eternity
of love
of softness
of quiet loving voice
inner voice
my true voice

Joy
Gratefulness
Harmony

Forgiveness has come

Relieved
freed from the burden
what a lightness
a new life unrestricted
a new law found
a calling
able to soar again

Come, my villain
come rest in my loving arms
come heal your broken heart
come feel the lightness
in every piece remaining

You are forgiven

And the mysterious willingness
out of my human heart
to run the risk
that betrayals hurting words
dark unbearable silence
may happen again again

Risk acknowledged
Risk taken

after all
Forgiveness

I do not remember
a life
without pain

My stomach area has always been painful, for as long as I can remember. This is how i was born.

I do not remember a life without pain.

I am tired of it. So tired of it. So tired of it. So tired of it. So tired of it. So tired of it. So tired of it. So tired of it. So tired of it. So tired of it. I have had enooooooooough....

Poisoning of self.
Because my body cannot process anything normally anymore.

Fibromyalgia. He said.
Spine distortion.
Nervous system blablabla
And more explanations I do, and do not understand.
They say
blablabla blablabla blablabla

This is enough for one person.
I am tired.
I have had enough.

I can endure a lot of pain,
I can endure so much.
In this way, I am unlucky.

I want to be weak sometimes,
I don't want to endure pain with a smile.
I don't want to be able to endure so much pain.

So much energy spent to keep this body standing.

I want to have a different relationship with my body.
One with no pain.

I want to be oblivious of the pain.

~~~~

I am a case, they marvel.

I don't want to be a case
I don't want to be special

I want to roll into a little ball
In a corner of the world

> And wait
> Do nothing
> Feel nothing
> Think nothing

~~~~

Drilling in my bones.
Grating in my bones.
Muscles being ripped off.
Nerves being pulled and pulled, deeply.
I am so weak.
My skin is on fire.
Intense cold in my bones.
Electric waves running through my body.
My blood becoming cement-like.
Spine nailed.

The Pleasures of the pain

What is there?
Who are you?

The reality of the other 'disease' is
not tangible.
Not visible.
Not understandable.
Inexplicable.

Isn't it terrific?
This is more difficult than a nameable disease.

Cancer? A piece of cake.

~~~~

I want to be **insouciant**

        carefree

if i am to live

I want to live,

                   instead of

     surviving

I have had

ENOUGH
!!!!!

I can't stand this body anymore.
My body can't stand itself anymore either.

I don't mind the pain.
I never wonder "Why me?"

But today I have had enough of this body.

Each cell,
each pore,
each part of the body,
is tired of itself.
They all want to scream.

I would like to get out of my body,
cut it savagely into hundreds of pieces,
and throw it away.

I just want a miracle now.
To stop it all.

Nothing less. A miracle.
Please.

~~~~

I create everything that happens to me
because I need it to grow.
Everything is here to serve me.
That is why I have nothing to fear.
Ultimately, **nothing can really hurt me.**
I am in charge.

Transformation and deep changes are so
powerful and phenomenal that the mind,
my little mind,
resists and is afraid.
Transformation and deep changes are great
but they don't always come easy.
What did you expect, little one?
A quick fix?

I know I will feel again and again,
the rebellion
and resistance of my little mind,
clinging to habits and what is known,
even if it is destructive.

I know I will want to give up
during low times.
To declare myself a shortage
of hope and strength.

I also know that I want
those transformations
and changes;
that I am making them happen,
even when I am crying and have had enough.

I must look quietly into
the depth of my heart,
and listen to the voice there.

Being wise being humble being patient
being compassionate with myself

To accept being tired, being limited,
being in pain
to let go
to surrender

Focus on what I can move
not what I cannot move
Focus on the strength I have
however infinitesimal

Only my mind or my ego, makes it difficult;
by wishing, regretting, comparing.

Outside of it, there is no problem

~~~~

Being a hero
is not about saving planet Earth,
it is not about having super powers.

Being a hero
happens in the thousands of simple acts
of my everyday life.

In accepting being myself,
being weak, slow, limited, revolted, calm:
in being myself totally.

Without faking or trying to be strong.
Without pretending or dwelling in pain,
and without the comfort of feeling
sorry for myself.
Without becoming a victim,
without complying in being a victim.

Being a hero
is to keep going on
in my little life,
day after day,
when everything goes berserk
and seems so hard.

And despite the odds, to keep SMILING

I am a little hero.

I am a hero of goofiness,
the queen of self-derision.
I am a tortue ninja,
the slowest one
in the world.
I move so slowly
that i might start
going backwards.
Here it is, for you,
a new dimension
of speed.
What else to say?
I am simply awesome.
I deserve a chocolate medal.

~~~~

If I imagine
the needs of my soul as my children,
I should honour them, listen to them,
respect them, help them grow and flourish.

They are the engine of my core.

I have taken care of my body,
my mind,
my inner desires.

Have I cared about them though ?

The food I eat,
does it satisfy my needs, my body?

Saying no, saying yes,
do I listen to my needs?

Accepting, resisting,
do I listen to my needs?

Changing, not changing,
do I take care of my needs?

Being considerate, humble, helpful,
non-judgmental,
do I listen to my needs?

Being joyful, smiling,
do I listen to my needs?

Slowing down, deciding fast,
contemplating, being aware,
do I listen to my needs?

Taking this path, is
it my needs?

physical spiritual mental emotional
energetic sexual financial personal needs

my values my body others Self

~~~~

it is a gift
to have happy shoes

my wisdom of the day

~~~~

La solicitude est parfois pesante.

They all tell me:

"Take care of yourself.
We want to keep you long"

"We need you"

"You are our sunshine.
Our wonderful Sunshine.
You have always been"

Love is a burden sometimes...

~~~~

Being

totally
truly

oneself

is scary

because

it is so deep
and

powerful
and

all-empowering
'

Few risk this path

~~~~

Je préfère crever de douleurs
que de perdre la tête

I'd rather die of incredible pain
than lose my mind

~~~~

the everyday life
doesn't feel like such
a survival today.
what a joy.

~~~~

Standing=painful.
Sitting=painful.
Sleeping=painful.
Breathing=painful.
Eating=painful.
Not eating=painful.
Moving=painful.
Being still=painful.
Dressing=painful.
Undressing=painful.
Taking shower=painful.
Walking=painful.

What's left?!?
Laughing=painful?
Painful or not, let's laugh softly...

My body is the smart one.
It leaves me with only one choice:
smiling or having a laugh.

I think any president of a country or every CEO
should be a body, not a mind. The world would
be so different if our bodies were governing us.

~~~~

Long ago, Women's body,
my body,
had been declared dirty, banned, rejected,
oppressed.
Because it is too close to the natural order of
Nature and its power.
Too close to the natural truth.

Men could not bear to have this power escaping
them. They could not bear their fear of not being
in control of this force. They could not bear to
admit their attraction to it.

So they make it dirty. Lower than theirs.

And this belief pervades the whole world up to
now.

In thousands of years, future generations will
look back at us and at our belief systems,
and they will wonder how we could have allowed
that, and how we could actually believe it...

~~~~

Since we lose everything
when we die,
we'd better give
everything
now

~~~~

My fear
seems like a beast.

Though when I look at it closer,
it is in fact just
a little thing,

trembling,
longing for love
and scared of being loved.

If I love my fear, will it disappear?

~~~~

I sometimes wish, deep down,
that this strange disease in my spine would be
fatal, and would lead me to death now.
Living is the hardest thing to go through
sometimes.
Living in pain, in a diminished state.
What kind of life is that?

Death is peaceful and calm.
Gentle.
Death means coming back home,
to my true essence.

Death is freedom.

Dying is lonely.
Exhausting.
Scary.
Slow.

...those thoughts are probably just
the rebellion
of the mind-ego.

~~~~

A major shift
is happening

Which feels like a huge wave.
Overwhelming.

Like a tsunami,
of Love and understanding.

A fantastic power.

I am self-healing

I am healing my Energy

Without warning, the wave suddenly started
from my toes and went all the way up.

It wrapped every single cell,
every part of my body.

This wave is an almighty force.
It is healing everything that it touches.
It is healing my Energy.
It is healing my body.

I can hardly allow myself to believe it.
Self-healing?
It is incredible.
Yet I know, I just know,
that this is what is happening.

It tastes….. how to describe it.
Words are too poor.

It is like manifesting what my intuitions knew.
It is like lifting the filter,
which was on top of my wisdom
in order to directly tap into it,
and use it.

I glimpse at the unbelievably awesome power
I have, that we all have,
in our physical body, our mind,
and our capacity to change, improve, heal.

In order to live the life we should have.

What a breathtaking, astounding out-of-mind
experience and sensation.

Bathing in this wave which has filled up my body.

Basking in this
water
light
presence
voice
nothingness
everythingness
no space
all space
no time

The cancer will be gone one day.
I know.
I know it.
Wiped out by this powerful wave of self-healing.
I won't need to go to the hospital to find out.

I just listen and trust my body,
my inner wisdom,
my higher self.

So easy.
So simple.
So beautiful.

Yes, healing can happen very quickly
Here and now
Right here right now.

Do not doubt
Do no doubt we have the capacity
To change
In radical ways.

~~~~

This time is
a PROMISE
for

FULFILLMENT
FLOURISHING
and
THRIVING

I am blessed
I am lucky
to be SICK

~~~~

I have nowhere to go
Nothing to do
No one to be

Except being exactly who I am
right now

~~~~

There is no loss
there is no gain, either
little one

~~~~

I died again.

My body became an empty shell.
No breath anymore.
My body was just an envelope.

This empty body-shell dissolved
with the senses.
Became
dust.
Ashes.

Only consciousness remained.

Consciousness in emptiness.
Not in an earthly sense.
Emptiness
in 'that which is devoid of
clinging-fear-matters-hope-past-future'
- kind of way

Emptiness in a beautiful,
whole way.
In silence.
In Energy.

Consciousness floating
Emptiness floating

Consciousness dissolving
into something bigger.
Deeper
Something I cannot name.

The rest of my dying experience,
I can't find words either to describe it.

Death,
An amazing moment of
Truth
Lightness
Beauty
and
Oneness

~~~~

BEING

AUTODESTRUCTIVE

sabotaging myself...

Could I also surrender to this?

A part of me wants to see how far I can go
into that
self-destructive part.

Into this refusal of life.

Into anti-healing.

Taboo subject. Shameful. Uncomfortable.

Aren't we all supposed to be happy
and choose life, they say?!

Where does it come from,
Being in suicide mode?

Stop
trying to understand, cure, heal, change —

Do I surrender or give up?
Is it wisdom or foolishness?
Is it equanimity or depression?

                    I long to become an amoeba again.
                              I long for home.
                              It is simple there...

" For when the mind is rested
there is no fight "

To find an answer,
ask the right questions first.
                                        Rest my mind.

Rest my mind
and answers will come faster.

The question is not how to trust,
but how much to trust.
                                        Rest my mind.

My fears are the seeds
of potential wisdom.
                                        Rest my mind.

The trap I must avoid is
to shrink from pain,
to become negative, bitter,
to stop the progression on the path.

                                        Rest my mind.

                    If the lotus grows out of mud,
                    i can grow something beautiful
                              out of this pain

                    ~~~~

When everything seems to go wrong,
instead of withdrawing,
let's go outward to others.

When everything seems to go wrong,
love, love more.

When I am sad
When I am lost
When I want to die
When I long for love

GIVE MORE - LOVE MORE

                    ~~~~

Today I feel very vulnerable
in a strong way.

I am very still inside.
I stand right in my center, in my core.

I am my Spaciousness.
I feel unshakeably calm.
Detached in an equanimous way.

My soul is in charge,
so to speak.

I feel a tremendous amount of compassion.
For every being, including my little self.

Because I see and feel their weakness
and struggles,
their pain and questions,
their wish for Love.
They are mine as well.
I understand it all. I know it.

Compassion is a peculiar feeling.

Such softness, yet such strength.
Such a 'drop down' to higher spheres,
a stripping down to essentiality.

Turning a hundred percent to others.
The ability to open my heart to others' pain.

A pause;
A profound pause into the truth
of what humanity means.

Totally letting myself being vulnerable.

And out of that vulnerability comes strength.

COMPASSION is LOVE
SO MUCH LOVE
which is
VULNERABILITY

COMPASSION
is not a feeling

It is a
STATE OF BEING

I am crying out of so much compassion and Love.
It is extremely beautiful.

~~~~

My brain, oh my brain,
shaking in all directions.
Expanding, then shrinking.
Permanent vibrations.

The space between my cells is blowing,
and blowing.

I feel the space between each cell.
I am there.

It is both pretty cool and unsettling.
I am living in my body at a cellular level.

I am inside my body,
and at the same time outside,
and I carry on with daily life.
Much concentration needed.

Could it simply mean
that I am losing my mind,
that I am truly becoming crazy...?

I do not care.
I do not want or need an explanation.
It is simply an phenomenal experience.

~~~~

Transformation
does not tolerate
mediocrity.

Here you are,
freshly baked thought of the day.
nearly as good as a croissant...

~~~~

Thank you trees. Thank you sea. Thank you air.
Thankyouthankyouthankyou...

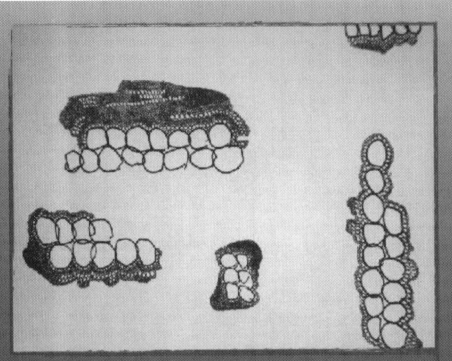

Game of the disease

Madness surrounds me now

.
..
...
...
... Here I am again indeed
Low times
Depression?

Just like I did with my pain,
I won't reject or won't feel ashamed
of this depression, but will totally enter it.

What if I love it?

Maybe i can hold it by the hand,
like a small, lost and sad child,
give it love, until love dissolves it.

I am not depression
I am not loneliness
I am not "wondering"
I am not pain

It might release the grip,
and the power it has on me.

Neither am I joy
beauty
calmness
laughter or growth

Remember, little one,
depression is just a dark side of me,
a pollution in my heart and my mind,
but it is NOT me — I must not identify with it.

I am all
and nothing

Those who have never experienced
depression or self-destruction
cannot fully grasp what it feels,
how powerfully it controls you,
and can ruin a life.

I guess I should also be grateful
to go through this?

Finding gratitude
in everything,
Can I do this when I feel so dark?

Depression might be the closest
to the truth humans are,
if there are not enlightened.

My body dances tonight.
It dances a shadow of a dance.
Dances at silent speed.
It dances a ghost of a dance.
Dances a slow dream of a dance.

Feeling my bones, muscles,
joints, fluids, organs,
moving
very slowly.

A little taste,
of ecstasy

I become ENERGY,
pure energy,
tipping down from my fingers,
down to my feet,
then to the ground.
Back to earth.

There is no more inside,
and outside in me.
There is no more skin,
no more body or shape.

I become lights,
I become colours,
I become transparent.
I am Energy.

I see the space between each cell
and the illusion of the body vaporizes.

I am everything indeed.
I am the whole.

I am love,
pure love

I dance

There is no more body
There is no more dance
My dance has no name
I am danced

There is no more question and doubt
No more pain and sorrow
No more happiness
No more body and stars
Because it is all the same

I dance

I am complete

Le Chant de mon Corps - The Song of my Body

Practicing having

NO HOPE
NO EXPECTATION
NO DISAPPOINTMENT
NO FEAR

with the return of the pain.

Back to square one it seems.

I know the geography of my body through the
pain, a very intimate map of my bones,
muscles, nerves and organs.

cement hollow bones
reverberating on muscles
awful courbatures - sore muscles
stomach area - painful again
skin - sensitive, burning, tingling, needling
muscles - stretched
femoral nerve - so painful
neck - crack, brittle - my neck could break
anytime
spine - the most painful of all, the deepest pain
of all
no periods for a very very long time –
am i still a woman?
between lightness and mammoth-heaviness

no communication with body anymore.

body why don't you talk to me?

Practicing having
no expectation, no hope.

I already know what it feels,
to be old and feel pain,
struggling to sit down, then struggling to stand
up, struggling to get dressed, struggling to
undress, going slowly from the bed to the
bathroom and back to the bed, sighing with the
least effort, dreading the least effort.
Dreading to get hurt, to miss a step, because it
would resonate in my whole body in painful
waves. Unable to carry anything.

Practicing having
no expectation, no hope.

I understand and feel so much for all the
elderly I see around me. I understand their
body and its weaknesses. The age difference
means nothing anymore; I am them.
I am a grandmother in a young body.

Maybe it is funny.
Grandma syv, better laugh at it.

~~~~

Be gentle with myself.

I have been super busy dying, surviving,
healing, suffering, cleansing, growing.

Watching my body and mind leaving, losing the
spark, the inner light, going down the drain.

Despite that, healing is still happening.
It does not mean curing is.

I watch with curiosity the process of dying.
Looking forward to be dead too, maybe.

...Yet not dying.
And feeling so depressed about being alive.
And in such a state of permanent wonder at the
same time.

So much darkness.
So much light.

Different stages Extreme stages
A full-time job A never-ending occupation

                    Going from

                      dying
                  to surviving
                   to living
                to surviving again

So, be gentle with myself.

It is only me here:
two hands. one brain. one breath.
one limited energy.

            I am close to nothing

And when I will have learnt everything
I need to learn from this experience,
will I be

                    HEALED

CURED

                              DEAD

                       ?

Not only does it take energy and effort to live
with pain, it takes up space as well.

Brain space.
Creative space.
Thinking space.
Constructive space.

Being in constant pain makes me shrink.
Not only physically, which is actually only a
collateral damage, an inconvenience.

What is harder is that I have
so little space left to think.
Pain is always here in my mind like a weight,
a fog, a bulk, an iceberg.

Thousands of 'simple' everyday life acts that
need to be adjusted and very carefully done.
Which also takes all my thinking potential away.

Being sick, being in pain
is such a constant burden.

A burden to be carried all the time everywhere.

What to do with it?
Talk about it? Keep silence?

It draws such an abyss between the healthy and
the sick. It makes me feel even more like an
alien among all those healthy people.

Pain or disease is like the elephant in the lift,
making it a challenge to enter the lift and go up.

Being sick and in pain is like having
an uninvited and
unwanted guest
in your living room.

You can accept it and not judge it.
You can put up with its behaviour,
you can even joke with it.
You can pretend it is not there.

Yet it is.

Nothing makes it vanish.

It is here, in your space,
eating your food,
watching tv when you want to sleep,
reading the book you want to read,
making a mess of your tidy space;
even inviting strangers in your safe space.

Day after day, all day long.

My options are then to walk around the pain,
grasp the limited space left over, live life from
that restricted world,
trying not to be crushed by the pain,
and its cortege of emotions.

I look around at people and I marvel
at how creative they are.

I, on the other side, feel so stupid.
No brain. No energy.

Pain is eating up my thinking creative space
It is eating up my clarity
It is eating up my brain
It is eating up my energy
It is eating up my joy
It is eating up my bones, my muscles
my inside and my spine

This is what annoys me the more I think:
having my mental,
creative thinking space
limited.

How to expand
within the shrinking?

And here again, the worst is not the pain.
The worst is not the limitations,
the shrinking.
The worst, is when I feel
LIFELESS.

It's not even being stiff like a wooden stick,
because wood is still alive, breathing:
having space inside.

It is more like being a cement pole.
Lifeless.
Spaceless inside.
Heavy and dense.
No breathing.

You see, being sick and in pain
is not fun,
but it is still a sign that
I am alive.

Pain itself is alive,
bursting,
moving,
expanding
and so on.

But this dreadful feeling of being
lifeless inside.
I cannot find words to describe it.

Eventually everything is comparative:
pain is quite cool after all.

There is always worse in
'the worst is...'
There are infinite layers...

~~~~

Celebration,

I can wash my feet in the shower without having
to sit down!

Champagne!

...though the day after:
a small death tonight, again I cannot reach my
feet in the shower, I need to sit down again.

Painkillers, I rarely take you, but today,
I love you.

Up and down up and down,
this is the process
of feeling better.

Which is when disappointment strikes the most -

thinking that I am getting better:
and realising I am not.

~~~~

We live in
the myth of
perfect health.

The myth that we must be totally healthy
all the time,
both in body and mind.

That if we are not,
there must be something wrong with us.

Can't we see how useful, beneficial and
obligatory disease is?

How could health exist without disease?

We forgot the principle of yin/yang
that governs all.

And in such, we also live in
the myth of
perfect happiness.

And with all comes the curse of guilt...

~~~~

Psoas muscles.

They embody our deepest urge for survival
and our elemental desire to flourish.
The Taoists call them the seat of the soul.

Little soul of mine, what are you telling me?

~~~~

Sick body
i love you
anyway

to live under
a Joyful, Bubbly & Colourful Sky
is very important

today's highly profound quote - i amuse myself so easily

~ ~ ~ ~

It is about

BEING

Being first,

then doing or having

How to fit
the ocean of questions
about the reasons
and purpose of Life
into the human limits?

Insane to try.

That is what I have been doing though.

I got insane.

Insanity of search,
of longing to understand.

The frustrations it brings.
The void.
The darkness.
The madness.

~ ~ ~ ~

My cells forgot who they were.
Or rather, they were not given
the right information anymore.

~ ~ ~ ~

Time to integrate traumas as well.
Big task.
Go slowly, be gentle with myself.

                          I cannot die well

            If I don't accept to live first

                                    Death = Life

How can I fully heal if,
at the back of my mind,
or my heart,
I still hold the thought that anyway
one day
I will commit suicide?

                              Lucky are you,
                      if you never have had
                      the thought of suicide

Body crushed
Body crushed from inside

i don't know anymore if this hurts
and how much

It is just too much

I've reached a state
where the pain
hurts so much
in many parts
of the body
that i don't know anymore
what i feel

My mind cannot
absorb anything anymore
or transcript into words
the body sensations

Self-preservation of the mind-
to step away from the pain?
to take a break from it?

Or too much pain
that took over
body and mind
and is deleting them?

My mind wanders
in an altered state
lost in a mist
where pain hides

Sometimes,
it is indeed
too much...

Even breathing has become

exhausting
and
painful

Debilitated
body

Strenuous
breath

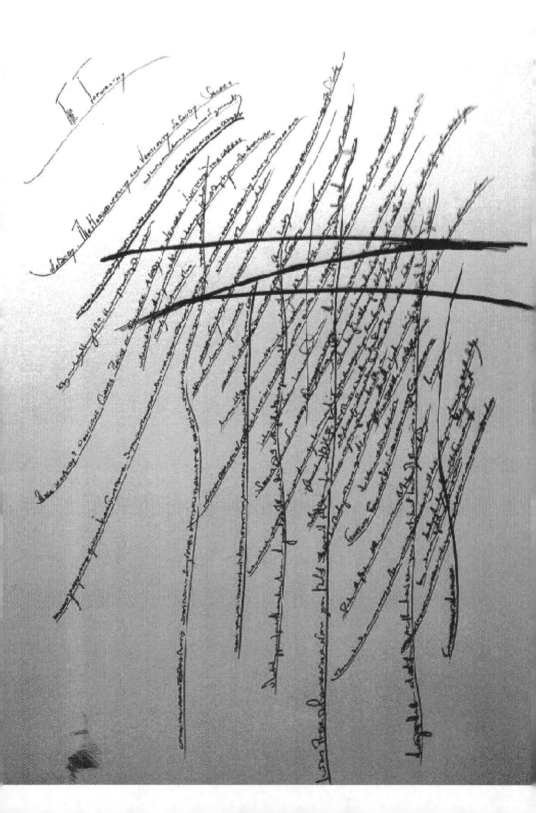

I dance again.
A little bit.
I can dance again.
Slowly. Just for a very short time. A few minutes.

When I dance,
I transcend pain and disease.

Dancing does not erase the pain:
it takes pain within,
and transforms it into creation.

I am my pain, dancing.
I am the dancer, watching my pain.
I am much more.

Pain is the background,
the air I lean against,
yet my fingers fly high.

Emotions, little mind, ego,
dissolve.

I am dancing

Thank you Thank you

My butoh dance
-like my drawings, poems and sculptures-

is a starting point
                    for reflecting
                    for questioning
                    for wondering

for myself and for the viewer.

I want the audience to question, ponder, reflect,
react, be repulsed, attracted, understand, not
understand, like or not, be uncomfortable,
delighted.

I want them to stop for a moment.

My dance is the starting point of their own
reflections and questioning.

Art is not a beautiful object to put on a
pedestal.
Art is supposed to make us wonder about life,
death, humanity.

My dance is not meant to be beautiful.
It is equally
not meant to not be, beautiful.

My dance is meant
to strike,
connect,
open a door.

And guiding students,
so rewarding and uplifting. I love it.
I love giving them time
and space to give birth
to their magnificence.

There is no more Syv, pain, mind, questions.
I become a presence, a holding space,
an act of giving,
a channel, a witness.

It brings me strength. Inner strength.
I receive as much as I give.

Thank you, students.

'The Space-in-between"

I suddenly found myself in a weird place
during a session of past lives regression.

The name that came to me naturally was

"The Space-in-between"

A space between lives

The first image or feeling was actually of space.
Endless.
Huge.
Eternity.

There was no limit, no boundary in that space.

It was dark in colour but not scary
and not dark because of the absence of light.

There was such a feeling of peace, quietness,
ease.

It felt so natural there.
It felt **home**.

I found myself floating in that space.
I had died and left my physical body.
I was just a spirit now.

I had some sort of shape though, as if wearing a
long triangular robe. But this shape or form was
more a mental image or feeling, rather than an
actual shape.
Actually it didn't matter which shape I had, or
whether I was a shape at all.
After all, I was a spirit.

When I looked around, I saw thousands of similar
shaped spirits, floating, as if hanging in space.

They were not moving.
I think they were resting.

When I said it was dark, it was more like a night
sky with millions of stars.
And i came to realise that these 'stars' were the
spirits, hanging.
As far as I could see, here they were, those
hanging spirits, lightly and peacefully floating,
blinking with soft light, resting.

I passed among them, floating.

Then I found myself next to a waterfall.
A very special waterfall.
It was not made of water.
It was made of energy.

I could see every single drop of energy which
made this waterfall,
every one, very clearly,
distinct from each other.
Millions of them separated and falling down
in a silent waterfall.
Shiny white. A special kind of white.
An energy white. A bit diamond-like.
Reflecting other tiny colours.
So shiny. Deeply. Subtle yet profound.

I know that this waterfall of energy is
pure knowledge,
pure wisdom,
pure love,
the essence of everything.

The **essence of me**.
This waterfall is also me.

Me as a spirit, made of this same energy.
So I am also knowledge, wisdom, love, essence.
I am it: and I am made of it.

The other spirits were made of the same energy
as well.
We were not matter anymore.
We were pure energy.

Such a wonder to be next to this waterfall.
To touch it.
I was my essence, watching myself.

Such a feeling of peace.
So much peace inside of me.
I was home.

Being home,
Being Love,
And being surrounded by Love.
Being peace,
And being surrounded by peace.
Being perfect,
And being surrounded by the perfection of the
moment,
the perfection of all.

The whole Space was bathing in

PURE LOVE

JOY

GROWTH

RESPECT

SUPPORT

Next I was surrounded by a circle
of **spiritual guides.**

One was a master. An advanced kind of guide.
He looked like the rest of us.
We actually all looked alike.
The master might have some distinctive sign,
but I could not 'see' , I could only feel.
But I knew, we knew, by watching each other's
energy, who was a master.

We were not talking with words either,
we were communicating through energy.
Such an easy flow of communication.

The spiritual master extended his hands towards
me and mine towards his.
He started to teach me.

That's how he was teaching, guiding me :
through our "arms" and the energy flowing
between.
An impressive amount of knowledge was given to
me, and i was absorbing it, naturally and easily.
By simply opening myself to learning,
information was coming, flowing, entering me.

The other spiritual guides were silently listening,
lovingly nodding, supporting me with their love,
agreeing silently.

This was
INITIATION
time.

For me to become a guide
in the future.

The knowledge came to me that actually
'next time' after I die,
I would not go back to earth,
but stay in the Space-in-between.

In order to guide other spirits souls.

I had gone through enough situations, emotions,
feelings, traumas during all those lives on earth.
I went through all of that in order
to know experientially,
and in my deepest memory what it was like,

to be tortured,
to be raped,
to love, and be loved, and lose the loved one,
to die, to be sick, to suffer in my body,
to run freely,
to rule and to listen,
to heal,
to have magic,
to see through truth
to give birth and to kill,
to feel hatred anger peace kindness joy
contentment forgiveness sadness.

So that I was ready to help and guide others.
It was all an initiation.

My **gift** is to heal.
My gift is compassion.
My gift is being sunshine.
My gift is having a healing love.

This is WHO I AM.

What an incredible feeling of
deep LOVE and JOY to know that.

I don't know how I 'know' this.
I just do.

...And I went there again,
in The-Space-in-between.

I had just died from torture in another life.

The spiritual guides were surrounding my dead body. I was watching myself – a dead body, and a spirit, at the same time.

It was
INTEGRATION
time.

I was watching my self -a body- with a lot of love and sadness, because I had just been through much suffering and my body had not been respected.

There was still much pain in that body.

I was watching it, taking all the pain in, softening it. Saying to my body that now it was recognised and respected.
That it could go in peace. Let go.

It was a deeply moving moment, watching my body being restored its right and purity.

Then this body slowly disintegrated and became ash, until all was dissolved and gone.

I floated away, more learning and initiations from the masters, were awaiting me.

...Another time when i went there, it was also deeply moving.

I was just about to be being sent to earth for this present life.

The guides, my masters and I were watching the life that I was about to go through, this very life i am in now.

There was silence and concentration, love and support around me.
Because we knew I was going to go through difficult times and some traumas, I would get sick and suffer in my body.

This was the path, the life I had chosen
in order to grow and learn more.

We knew it would not be easy.
So we were all watching with respect, silence and support.

Earth is just a level, a part of our spiritual life.

We all have different gifts.
We are all at different levels of growth and knowledge.
It does not matter where we are on our growth journey, and in our evolution.

We all respect and support each other.

There is no competition in
the Space-in-between,
neither better or less.

When one spirit grows and learns,
it is the whole community of spirits
who benefits from it.

Because there is no separation.
WE ARE ALL ONE

So I don't grow only for myself.
I learn and evolve for everyone.

~~~~

Even when I am weak, sad, empty,
so tired and in pain,
I realise that
I am still strong for others.

I possess an unshakable inner strength
to take them all into my arms,
and comfort them.

Nothing can hurt me.
Because I am Love.

~~~~

We are spiritual beings first.

Then we are a body.
All the negative emotions come from our
forgetting it.

Behind each person,

even a murderer, or a rapist,
an ignorant or ugly one,
a selfish or loving one,
a mean or giving one,

is a soul.

All my dying experiences are about Life,
not death.
They also are a messages of Love.

I am here to live Life fully,
to reach my highest potential,
whatever it means,
to love, to create,
to give and receive,
to laugh and cry,
to expand and grow,
to fail and succeed.

Negative emotions
can never be justified
because
they are not needed.

Anger is not needed.
Despair is not needed.
Hatred is not justified.
Cruelty is not justified .
Selfishness is not needed.

Of course I am worthy.
I am a spirit. How coud I not be worthy?

...and I am already complete.

Unconditional Love

is

our essence

Our soul

is

PLAYFUL

Being in constant pain keeps me grounded
for sure!
Anchored in the human experience.

Was it a way for me to become grounded,
for someone without a base, or a home?
I never choose the easiest path.

Being in constant pain helps me to be focused.
To be aware.

> *Hey, everyone should have*
> *a pretty little nasty disease.*
> *It's the highway for growth*
> *and realisation.*
> *The thing is that you can't really choose*
> *your disease,*
> *you cant pick it up from a catalogue.*
> *Too bad.*
> *The system is flawed.*

Being in constant pain does not make me a superior
person. Even if others often complain and make a
big deal out of a tiny amount of pain.
They suffer at their level, at the level they are
and need to be.

Being in constant pain does not give me the right to
judge them or dismiss their pain.
I do not truly know how much they can endure,
what and why they need to endure,
and which level of pain is a challenge for them.

I receive what I can handle.
So do they.

There is always someone who suffers much
more than me and could consider my pain as
a holiday trip. I know I would appreciate their non-
judgmental love and support towards
this little pain that is mine.

So I should give to others the same
non-judgmental love and support
towards their little ounce of pain.

> What I wish to receive
> I should give first

~~~~

Fear governs us all first and foremost.

Who decided to create human being that way?
Weren't there other choices and tools to make
our souls grow?

What a wicked choice...

I don't "fight for" or "fight against".

Too much energy required,
too much energy wasted.

I am in the "building" and "creating".
I want to use my energy to build and create
which feels more uplifting and calls for positive
changes.

~~~~

Cocktail Recipe

Take a bone
sprinkle it with laugh
Add a pinch of nonsense
and two ounces of love
Shake well
Pour in a martini glass
and enjoy

à boire sans modération

~~~~

The 8-pm supermarket experience

Filled mainly with corporates of all kind –Singaporeans,
foreigners, males, females- singles, some families.
All desperate to get it done quickly.

I am watching the ones very focused, heading straight to
the needed items.
The ones browsing the aisles, what's for dinner tonight?
The ones totally absent, eyes, mind and body glued to
their i-phone.
Most of them looking tired.

Then come the long lines at the register counter.
Impatience. Stress. Pressure.
From and for the customers. And the staff alike.

I watch the purchase of my fellow human beings:
The woman behind me - only frozen food
Behind her a guy with beer snacks processed food
At the next counter, a basket of fresh vegetables, fruits
and eggs for a woman
Another one of canned food and toilet paper

And the plastic bags experience!
so shocking in Asia

One plastic bag for the toothbrush
One plastic bag for 2 tomatoes
One plastic bag for the can
Two plastic bags for the melon

What a waste. Hello people?!?
How can you waste so much?

It sounds weird, but for me the supermarket experience
is always fun and exciting. Much to learn about a country
and its eating culture. I slowly walk the lanes like a
spectator of a movie. I don't actually need to buy
anything, maybe I am looking for a distraction from my
pain.

Here in the supermarket, I also wonder
who is really the sick person.
If those people are healthy, why do they look so
miserable?

~~~~

THE SECOND

HEALINg

wAVE

is happening now.

This time is not physical.
It is not about healing pain and disease.

This time its about

EXPANSION

After so many months where
i felt being eaten up by the disease
and the constant pain
watching my thinking creative
space vanish, occupied by the reality of dealing
with the pain

a different process is happening

I still have pain
however it does not matter anymore.

Because my mind, my thoughts, my creativity -
are expanding.

I finally feel
the VASTNESS
of my inner mind
and thoughts.

I finally managed to jump beyond the pain -
the pain itself, the idea of the pain, the
knowledge of the reality of the pain, the
uncertainty about the origin of this pain,
and whether I would feel it forever-
which was occupying my space.

And I found more space beyond.

Ahhh, what an epiphany!
What a delight!

I can think again
            I can dance again
I can create again
            I can imagine again

Thank you!

The ecstatic taste, and feeling
of my brain expanding.
A wonderful experience.

~~~~

Tenderness,
don't forget tenderness.
much needed.

~~~~

I often feel I don't belong to this time on earth, where it is all about $$, power, connections, profit, recognition, having, accumulating.
I don't fit into this mentality, into what prevails and runs this world.

How come people are appreciated and considered successful according to what they do, how much money they make, what is their latest mobile or car, how big their house is, or where they live? Not according to who they are, how close they live to their essence, how much they benefit others.

I don't fit in this world, where I must pay sg$1,000 for a room. Just a room. Or be in debt for 30 years to have my own house.

Maybe I belong to another century?
To another realm?

I don't think life was easier before. Life was probably more simple. Being wealthy or not probably also made a difference then, but maybe there were alternative systems which were also working -'I do this for you, in exchange you do this for me'.

Now only money is ruling.

I think many people have much to offer beyond money. Many want to share what they know, who they are. And cannot because the system does not allow them this simplicity, this natural way of living.

In some countries, they have been living a joyful life with nothing to miss so far. Then people suddenly realise -or rather, are told- that they are poor and backward. According to which standards? According to some western highly-developed countries' index?

Now they compare themselves with a society thousands miles away (and worse, a distorted image of this society) and feel poor, backward, stupid.

How sad.

We make everything more and more complicated, with more rules and regulations, do's and don'ts.

We poison ourselves, we poison earth, we poison meaning.

More and more people run: run through their lives. They must look busy and productive, in order to exist. To have a role and a meaning. It is not advisable to have too much free time. To go slowly.
Better to forget oneself by running. Better to forget how to understand or even know oneself.

How sad.

People don't know what they want, or worse, who they are, because they never stop. They need more, more, more.

It does not make sense to me. Simplicity is not highly regarded these days.

I look at the world around me, and see so much distress. Right in our faces or hidden under the veneer of a luxury life. So much unhappiness in many forms. And people keep running, to escape the reality of this misery.

Is this how we are supposed to live?
Who have we become?
How much have we lost ourselves?

How did we forget, that we have a choice, always.
That we have power.

How did we forget, to trust ourselves, and our infinite possibilities?

How much have we lost sight of what is ESSENTIAL?

Oh, Man, what have we become?

I don't believe we are meant to live this rushing life.
I believe we are meant to see beauty around us.
We can devote time to learn new skills purely for the interest and passion of it.
We can exchange our skills and knowledge in a more human, and equal way.

And I don't mean to go back to Stone Age. I mean just stop being caught up in the acquisition of things, titles, justifications.

Just slow down first.
Stop, to look at yourself.
To go back to simplicity.

Beyond the necessity of me resting my bones and the reality of being sick, I hold the belief that I am happier this way, by slowing down, being closer to what is essential, peeling off and discarding what I don't need. And I need little.

We need little.

I do not reject modern life. I simply disagree with some aspects of it, and do not buy the by-products of negativity, materialism and consumerism it creates.

I do not want to follow this voice.
I do not want to be polluted – mind, body, soul – by today's world.
I want to embrace my values and my core, and not have to spend energy to protect myself against a destructive environment.

Planet earth looks so retarded to me sometimes. Technology is not necessarily a sign of advancement.

There are so many more ways to be happy and fulfilled, more than the society wants us to believe, and follow.

There will come a day when all this becomes too much; too powerful for our own mind and reasoning, too overwhelming for our small human condition.

We will either have to get rid of it all, of our lifestyle and way of thinking, or it will get rid of us...

~~~~

STOP being adventurous
Stop offering other choices, little one.

Because eventually people always go back to their comfort zone, whether it is an ice-cream flavour or dance.
They taste for a minute, this unusual new flavour. They might even like it.
But they won't buy it.
Vanilla or chocolate, : still safer.
It's the same with movements,
and everything else.

It is not easy to be a pioneer.

I know that one of the reasons why Oneness Flow, the movement healing technique I am trying to set up, and Butoh, might never work.
Because it is not fun.
It is not striking.
It is not a distraction.
It is the BIG QUESTIONS.
It is about you. you asking the big questions.
Searching for some truth.

People want entertainment, sparks, fireworks.

They want a show.
They want results. NOW.

~~~~

I think sex

is the ultimate earthly chance

to experience

our selfless,

egoless,

timeless

and shapeless

Higher Self

or soul

~~~~

The question is not

"do I love?",

but

do I deny
someone

the possibility
to love me
?

~~~~

Good morning little birds,
thank you for being here

~~~~

WHY DID I CHOOSE TO LIVE

?

Why
are we
so afraid of
GROWING
?

Surrendering

and **accepting**

the **AUTO-DESTRUCTIVE**

side of me

Not pushing it away.

This side is an aspect of my life,
together with love, wonder and amazement.

Another aspect I have been given to experiment,
just like the pain, being sick, dying, being happy.

I don't want to run away from this learning.
Not that I wish to be miserable.
These two perspectives are different.

I look straight at its many faces, embrace it, in
order to understand it, with my heart, body and
mind, energies and cells memories.

I am still alive
in order to explore
this self-destruction
with a new awareness.

It is the twofold learning experiences
of this life time:

pain-disease-dying,
and self-destruction-suicide

Fully accepting this self-destruction,
is not denying life.

It means living fully,
all aspects of life;
not only the easy and beautiful ones.

So here you are, little one,
more digging to do.

Oh dear, this is not easy.

Suicidal thoughts,
what can i tell you?

Can I embrace suicide
in order to learn what is beneath it,
to understand the reasons behind it,
then kill myself?
or not kill myself?

How can I embrace suicide
without committing suicide?

Self-destruction,
do you want to talk to me?

What are you screaming or whispering?

i am listening

I feared living before,
because I was longing to end this life.
I was longing to go back to my spirit form.

I did no accept living before;
I could not keep on living without seeing
the bigger picture,
without understanding the ultimate meaning
and reason of life.

                    There is no meaning to Life.

I did no accept living before
for the mere sake of it,
for a decision of some far away god
or the universe scheme.
I searched and searched
for the meaning to life.

                    There is no meaning to Life.

I wondered how
we could possibly accept
this absence of meaning.
How we could not be startled
by this highly aberrant situation.

                    There is no meaning to Life.

I hit a wall, again and again.
Refusing to surrender,
to accept such a nonsense.

                    There is no meaning to Life.

I run and run
like a wild headless bird
in a mad circus.

                    There is no meaning to Life.

How can i keep on living
if there is no meaning to life?
Why should I live one more day
if there is no meaning to life?

I got lost.
I became silent rage,
fists fighting a desperate and helpless battle.
I got insane
mind exploding
under the fireworks of destructive bullets.

Mind muting into its own bullets.
Self-destruction
coming over me.

                    There is no meaning to Life.
                    There is no meaning to Life.

I dreamed of a saviour
who would explain it all to me.
The saviour never came.

                    There is no meaning to Life.

I got stuck,
entangled in the bundle of wires
that my mind had become.

                    There is no meaning to Life.

My guts screamed, rant and raved.
Revolted I was.
In despair.
Too big of a question for my little mind.

                    There is no meaning to Life.
                    There is no meaning to Life.
                    There is no meaning to Life.

I shut myself
to stop this deadly quest.
I shot myself
right in the core.
And buried the remains of my soul
in a meaningless life,
under the rubbles of my war zone self.

                    There is no meaning to Life.

I expelled my body
from its existence.
There are many ways
to stop the reality of a body,
to discard it.

                    There is no meaning to Life.

I refused to have a body
-and i still do-
Body, I don't want you,
such a cumbersome vessel,
such a burden.

Nothing personal, body.
I just don't want a body.
I want to fly, be light,
I want to vanish.
I want to be thin air.
I want to be my spirit self.

                    There is no meaning to Life.
                    There is no meaning to Life.

I don't want to live on earth.

                    There is no meaning to Life.

I don't want a body.

                    There is no meaning to Life.

I don't want to live.

                    There is no meaning to Life.
                    There is no meaning to Life.
                    There is no meaning to Life.

I want to die.

                    There is no meaning to Life.
                    There is no meaning to Life.
                    There is no meaning to Life.
                    There is no meaning to Life.

Let me die.

                    There is no meaning to Life.
                    There is no meaning to Life.

                                    There is no meaning to Life.

                                                When will I die?

                                    There is no meaning to Life.
                                    There is no meaning to Life.

                                                Let's die...

I am a CHILD in AWE
in front of Life, Nature, Mystery

I am a SIMPLE SOUL
deeply tasting it all, marvelling
and being grateful.

I am a DARK DESTRUCTIVE FORCE
challenging, pushing the limits of
my body and self

I am LIFE
both holding the yin and yang
the positive and negative
the light and the darkness
the constructive and destructive

I used to think it was a curse
to be depressive,
to have these destructive thoughts
and behaviours.

I might see it now as a blessing:

I hold these two extremes
with equal proportion
to allow me to totally understand them.

An end is near.
I know.
the end of my body?
the end of my blindness?

sometimes it is just dark…

~~~~

a wounded,
unwanted
child -

depression.

a lonely
child,
longing for
love -

my pain.

~~~~

It is pretty amazing, how much resilience
and strength humans display,
and find in themselves to endure -
deep pain, wars, losses.

And to stand up again.
And keep going.

Humans.
Quite a mystery.

~~~~

Welcome back, dear pain

                        I asked them,
                   the different pains,
           where they had gone for a while.

           They answered that they died.
                            A little bit.

                         Some vanished.
           Some were swallowed into the abyss.

           They rested. They waited.
                        Then woke up.
                        They are back.

Opposite notion of compressing and pulling out.
That is how my pelvis hips back and spine feel.
Encased in a steel armour.
And being pulled by mad strings.
Not so pleasant.

Me in the middle, watching.
                        Am I the referee?

The pain is back again, and this time I can
handle it. Can I?
I am not sure which direction it is taking me -
will it mean a healing/curing/respite time/
worsening?

It does not matter much to me.

This time I decided to deal
with this pain and self-destruction
ALONE.

No nutripuncture, no energy healer, no
alternative treatments.
Only butoh and digging.

I have been here before.
I need to search deeper in order
to understand it all
— in my flesh, my bones, heart,
mind and ego.

If I run away today, I will not be able to
understand it or wake up from it.
Or if I look for ways to give a milder tone to it.

I am not calling pain for the sake of it,
I am not a victim.

I only want to understand;
to dig deeper into my darkness and
find out more.
to transform pain into joy and love.
to wake up from the dream of life and find
reality.
to finally hear again, the totality of the voice of
my soul, not its mere whispers.

It is far from being easy everyday.
Yet, in the silence and loneliness of my self,
I am trying, day after day, to go closer to my
truth.

It is hard sometimes
to find the physical energy and strength
to keep searching.
My mind can be weak and lures me into laziness.
My body is often weak and leads me to bed.

I find out so many new "the worst is..." during
this whole process.

I used to think that the worst was the pain.
Then I realised that the worst was actually being
eaten up by this pain and sickness,
and having no more space for creativity,
thinking, being.

Now I feel the worst is to always be exhausted.
There are days when I feel so lethargic,
I have no energy to even write a few lines.
I can only lay in bed. Mornings are hard.
Such an effort to get up.

Body weak,
body crushed,
breath not helping anymore.

How do I summon energy to go beyond this
lethargic state and tiredness, to research?

How do I summon energy to go beyond this
lethargic state and tiredness, to dance the pain
in order to find answers?

This is the trick I need to learn.

Of course, I also occasionally
wish to have a different body,
to have a fluid
and flexible body,
an obedient and easy body.

I want to jump, twist, bounce.
I cannot.

So I must create another dance
from my painful spine.

What a wonderful chance
to research
this dance
of a limited body,

to know, feel, taste,
reach deeper,
than if I was healthy.

I still can create infinite options
if I move beyond
the limitations
of my mind.

I am so

blessed

~~~~

Being able to breath
is Joy

Breathing is a miracle

Such a world in one breath

~~~~

We are so scattered.

We look like puzzles with missing pieces.
Or a smashed mirror.

We don't know who we are anymore.
We hide.

We have contracted.
We have become a blurry image of ourselves.

~~~~

Body not responding to the natural course.
Body stops being obedient.

My body becomes an alien to me.
My body is a box of surprises.

Not the most pleasant gift.

~~~~

I am a skeleton walking, moving
clac clac - my bones, squealing, drilled and
crushed
my nerves screaming like a punk concert
my neck grinding a cracking symphony
my skin burning, itching
my stomach dead, bugged
my spine, a total broadway show
my muscles, permanently bungee jumping
my mind - an absolute drama queen

so much fun, right?

~~~~

Can I find peace in Life?

Can I find peace in living?

Can I find peace in being alive?

-maybe-

I have been wishing to die for so long

Two opposite directions meeting in one,
and trying to reach a balance,
however contradictory it might seem.

Little by little,
I might find some peace
in being alive…

~~~~

If I was looking at my pain
as an enemy,
I would reinforce the ego,
who wants to see itself
as a victim.

If I was fighting the pain,
I would assume, from my ego's point of view,
that the pain was wrong and the ego was right;
that the pain was external and the ego was
above it.

My essence is
neither right nor wrong
and the pain is part of it.

Though this pain is not it either.

~~~~

For most people, there is a lot of
guilt
in acknowledging, and accepting
the imminent
death
of a loved one.

We still have a long way to go,
to a more natural reaction towards death.

So many people would die peacefully
if their loved ones could accept
this most natural event:
their death.

Doctors!
Death is not a failure.
It cannot be avoided.
It is the only sure end we know.
Let go of another ultimate treatment.

Accept and embrace death.

~~~~

Treasure the moment, this very moment.

How could I not give the best to people,
if it was my last breath?
How could I not give them smiles, love,
support, respect to who they are,
if this was my last act?

Every second could be the last one.
How wonderful it all becomes,
from this perspective.

~~~~

I look at my little self
as a child
who needs guidance, reassurance,
and above all,
who needs
Love

~~~~

... I become my pain

                                                  And I burst into tears

I feel love and compassion for this pain which does not know anything else, but to hurt me –

I become my pain and I dance

I am the pain in my hips and in my legs, this grating and drilling sensation –
I ask my pain "What do you want to do?" –
the answer comes as obvious :

"I want to spread. I want to go as far as I can in your body. I want to have fun.
I want to kill you. I want to hurt you. This is what I am."

I become my pain and I cry

I become my pain, and I dance and I smile and I feel joy

                                -I am my pain, dancing –

I am a pain experiencing beauty -How could I ask pain to do anything else but to hurt me –
this is solely its goal, and meaning
Yet I am pain, experiencing beauty

                              - I am beauty contained in pain -

I feel blessed

blessed to have **Butoh,**
and to be able to search my body and pain through the dance,
to reach deep darkness

                                        - I am blessed I have Butoh and I sob -

I have been going right into the pain.
Or taking it into my Spaciousness,
and feel it from there.

But tonight I thought:

**How about I transfer
my Spaciousness
into the pain?**

What a massive difference.

Instead of being in pain in my Spaciousness,
the world of the pain
takes the dimension of my Spaciousness.
But in front of such vastness,
the pain suddenly becomes so small,
so insignificant.

There are no walls, no boundaries,
no limits anymore,
where it can bounce off and hurt.

What can the pain do?
Only dissolve.

If I look further into my body
at a cellular level, at an energy level,
what has pain become?

Empty space

Lots of empty space around the cells,
inside the cells.

The pain has nowhere to grab on anymore.

If my bones, my nerves, my muscles, my organs
'dissolve' or 'disintegrate' as only energy,
there is no support anymore for the pain to hold
on to.

What a major discovery for me.
To be able to truly watch the pain that way.

~~~~

LAUGHTER!!

I love laughing

I need to laugh more

Living life at my cells level.
What an extra-ordinary
state and journey.

i am fluid
endlessly pulsating
expanding my soft skin
to gather strength
contracting to retain
the tasty sustenance

i am water
an ocean of aliveness
infinitesimal unit of life
-your life-
yet fundamental
in strength and meaning
every part of me holds
life and its necessity
a prodigious treasure
silently breeding
innumerable cosmos

I am nucleus
drumming
a far-away earthquake
contained in your fluidity
making my voice
resonate like a thunder
an almighty echo
deafening in your ears

i am plasma
vibrating
together with
the trillions of sisters
surrounding me
we are one
gently brushing each other
in ceaseless embrace
living for each other
breathing through each other

I am a slimy liquid
quivering
and each shiver
reverberates in the darkness
of your body
sending a myriad
of furtive messages
through hidden passage ways
in unspoken languages

I am countless tiny cubicles
breathing
as the same tempo
as your heart beat
forming a miraculous duo
singing the song of life
my inbreathe rises
as high as a mountain
my microscopic cell peaks
bring vertigo
to your senses
who lost all perception of scale

i am fluid
listening to the universe
of your body
responding to the tides
which govern
inner and outer infinities
caressing your bones
nourishing your thoughts
whispering to your desires

i am fluid and matter
and know who you are
more than you do
i have been bestowed
the home keeper
of past and future
my water contains
the memories of All
moulding your future
in secrecy beyond
your understanding

I am a cell
pulsating and vibrating
drumming and breathing
stretching and shrinking
creating and seeding

I am your cells
whose rhythm
has been altered
by a mysterious invader
thrown into
unknown territory
trembling at the edge of
your new world order

i am your cells
pulsating
vibrating
drumming

and you can hear me

*I don't remember
what it is to bounce with energy,
to take the body for granted
because I wouldn't feel it,
because it is not hurting
and is not tired.*

Today my hips and pelvis are caught in an iron cast again, with two powerful iron hands digging deep into my bones and muscles.

Bring my Spaciousness in there....
Bring them into my Spaciousness -
Exhaustion all over my body and mind...

I wish sometimes I was not so resilient and resistant,
I wish I was weak and not able to handle much pain.
What a curse.

I still can smile through my pain.
What a curse.

I store in my body the memory of pains.
Pain from right now.
Pain from my ancestors.
Pain from previous lives.

So much pain.
So many memories stuck inside of me.
Feeding on more pain and traumas.
Calling for them.
Creating more to survive.

The necessity to break the cycle,
this endless hell.
The necessity to break those memories free,
and harmless.

If I dance them,
i can transform them into creation.
Can I?

If i love them,
and give them a way to express themselves,
they will disappear.
Will they?

All is dark.

**What can I create
from this darkness?**

I WISH

I HAD DIED

when I was so weak.
I wish so much I had died.
I am alive unfortunately.
All is dark.

Retour en arrière. Back to many years ago.
Similar process. Other defence.
Running in circles?

The weakness of the mind and the fault of being human.
The desperate cry of a soul trapped
in a body shape, and a limited mind.

The outcry of a mind who wish for
and feels more but fail to perceive
the Understandable, the Mystery,
the reason and meaning for all.

The despair of a body who holds the truth,
the memory of 5-billion year old cells,
whose opinion and wisdom
is not asked for.

What a sad description of human beings.
Of myself.
It breaks my heart.

Running in endless circles and holding on
desperately to the little we know and feel,
mistaking what we possess,
for the ultimate truth and achievement.
What else could we do?
Are we given another choice?

All is illusion,
illusions are all we are making.
It should bring comfort to know it is only illusion.
Sometimes it doesn't.
We should rejoice to know that all is an illusion.
We don't.

i dont know i dont know i dont know i dont
knowidontknowidont

~~~~

if I was
living
in a high-storey building,

could I reach
the top

tonight,

climb over the rail

and

let myself

fall

?

I realise I've lost my smile.
No laughter, no smile inside.
No smile on my lips.

I watch myself.

Only silence.

Time suspended.

Body and mind suspended.

Silence and emptiness inside.

Even the mind has stopped
to run in endless circles.
Even the mind is silent.

There is only 'be':

The 'be' a tired body
The 'be' a tired Syv
The 'be' a sad alone one
The 'be' beyond words
descriptions and reasons

I am experiencing the 'being'

I am weakness, flaws and failures
I am joy, i am tenderness, I am sunshine

Becoming **RAW**.

Hiding nothing.
Letting go of excuses and explanations.
Becoming raw.
An open heart.

Being there,
at this pure place or rawness,
is very vulnerable.
To be so open and honest.

It is also incredibly beautiful, and peaceful,
and gives me amazing strength.
I get prodigious strength
from this purity,
from this clarity.

This strength is
forgiving and
loving,

it is all-mighty,
powerful beyond measure,
and silent.

It can handle everything.
It is limitless.

This strength is
me.
A child of the Universe.

I melt in front of my self-child.
I have so much Love.
I am Love.

I am

FORMLESS,

And every form.

I am prior to forms,

I am beyond forms.

I know nothing

I am a clear slate

You know, feeling peaceful.
Just be.
Just is.
Just now.

The immediate reality of my happiness.
Focus on it.

~ ~ ~ ~

There is no glory in being sick.
There is only pain, limitations,
loss and loneliness.
Understanding and joy as well.

There is no glory in recovering either.
None of this, defines me.
it is just a part of the whole,
a part of the journey.

~ ~ ~ ~

I am alone

in so many aspects of my life.

There is a lot of freedom in being alone.

There are a lot of responsibilities as well.

And it requires much energy and strength.

~~~~

The true learning is in daily life.
Not in books.
You have to put it into practice at some point.

~~~~

I am a simple mind.

Who doesn't like too many words
(yet is writing now, isn't it funny?).
Who doesn't like to analyse and intellectualise
too much.

Because I believe it kills the Truth.

The Truth of who I am is very simple.
Maybe no explanation can convey that level of
simplicity.

The game of talking and analysing comes from
the little mind.
Who wants to look smart.
And is scared of the simplicity
of the Truth of who i am,
and of my Spaciousness.

The simplicity and the small things,
are the songs of the Universe,
of Awareness.

The simplicity and the small things,
hold enormous power.

To be attuned to them,
in a state of oneness,
is a joy.

Very smart and cunning, this little mind.
Very primitive yet powerful.
This little mind of ours also perceives
negativity as pleasure, feeds on it and makes us
believe that it will get us everything.

Hey, guys, upstairs, in the Universe,
what's the hell of an idea you had
to create us like that?!

What a world, this Earth.
I can't wait to get to another universe.

~~~~

Nature
is the connection with Pure Love,
with awareness.

Nature is the door to my soul.

Nature is the understanding of
Perfection-as-the-way-it-is.

Nature is the manifestation of
the Universe consciousness.

Nature is me and I am Nature.

How unselfish and giving Nature is.
Nature gives without counting;
such incredible beauty, creativity, wisdom,
presence, humour.
Asking for nothing back.

Nature is so healing and humbling.
And SIMPLE.

In front of Nature everything becomes so
simple indeed,
so clear and obvious.

I am a child in front of Nature.
I am Nature's child.

In nature I come back to
my own rhythm,
my true nature,
my true Self.
Which is nothing.

IT IS.
Only that.

Nothing else is needed in a world
surrounded by Nature.

if i don't die and get more strength,
i am going to live in nature.
No postponing anymore.

~~~~

<div align="right">

**I already live
my ideal life**

it is just a matter of fine tuning it,
entering into more details and layers.
it is pretty cool.

</div>

~~~~

Live fully to have no hope,
as hope comes out of fears and regrets.

And let go of my attachment to fears too...

~~~~

And of course, I also fail to be aware. I forget my breath. I forget to take a step back. I forget my Spaciousness. I want to be who I am not. I want a flexible body. I want what I don't have. I want a human spiritual teacher. I want an easier life. I want someone to take care of me. I want someone to take my hand. I want someone to show me the way. I want a car with a driver because I am too tired for buses. I want to travel. I want to stop worrying about money. I want nice underwear. I want my sister to feel better. I want my mom to surrender and find her self. I want to play laugh talk make love. I want a big bed where I can stretch. I want to be in the mountains. I want an ice cream kiss. I want to walk without pain. I want to surrender more. I want to stop wanting. I want I want I want.

Stop wanting.
Leave the ego.

Then I laugh.
I don't want anything.
I don't need anything.

How to keep living, breathing, dancing,

or
simply being,

when cancer and a strange
nervous system disease
-and the pain that comes with it-
take over my body and my mind,
drill, grate, penetrate bones, muscles, nerves?

When the whole space of thinking, creating,
humouring, moving
is eaten up by the pain and those
invisible entities?

I become silence.
I enter the body.
I slow down.
I become a possessed body.

I become the pain
and the sick cells,
my own killing creation
from within.

They know nothing else but hurting, killing,
spreading: this is their sole purpose, why should I
ask them to have sympathy for me?

So I give them space to express themselves,
to scream their fears and longing,
their meaning, their despair and their hope,
their life-on-their-own.
I tell them 'I love you'.
They dance my body.

When the body is too difficult to carry,
I become
more silent,
just one breath at a time.
Such a world in one breath.
I slow down more.

I become raw.
Raw bones.
Raw pain.
Raw darkness.
Raw priorities.

I taste death and its beauty,
i taste simplicity and softness.

I go back into my mother's womb.
I search in my darkness, deeper and deeper,
no words needed to find some truths.
The body knows.

I taste Life with wonder.
Every single action is fabulous.

I am lost sometimes.
I don't know who I am anymore,
I lose my mind.
Dreadful.

I am so tired.

                                    I become estranged
                                          from my body.

I want to have a flexible strong unlimited body.
I want to have brilliant ideas
and a creative mind
like others around me.

I want to be who I am not right now.
Stop wanting.

Go within.
Be the pain.
Don't miss this chance.

                                    I become
                        thousands of universes.
                                    There is
                                    no more
                        inside and outside.

I find many edges, so many.
I feel so limited.
I try to keep my smile and joy,
sometimes i succeed,
sometimes I fail.

And when the pain and disease
go away briefly,
like a tide,
giving me space to dance and create,
I taste Life with awe.

Pain and disease are great teachers.
They are blessings in disguise.
I am grateful.

Slowly,
I try to transform them
into my own creation,
my own dance.

I imprint
this intense and deep experience
in my body.

Infinite dances to come.

AND WHAT ELSE

IS THERE

ANYWAY,

TO ACHIEVE -

BESIDES LOVE?

THE PAIN

Struck me unexpectedly

All kind of pains
All at once
Everywhere
Extreme pain

pain in my bones, in both arms and legs
pain in all my nerves
pain in the back muscles
pain all along the spine
deep deep pain, in my lower spine
pain in my stomach
strong headache behind the eyeballs

It was the most severe, and worst pains,
I had ever felt over the last 12 months.

I thought i had experience pain
— I hadn't yet, at that level.

My pelvis was so overwhelmed with pain,
that I didn't feel my legs anymore:
I fear to be paralysed.

I could not stay more than a few seconds in one
position in my bed. No position brought comfort.

It felt a bit like being knocked over by a truck,
and before I could catch my breath,
pause and realise what was happening,
another truck would knock me down,
drive over my body;
then another, and another.

I could hardly breathe.

No more thinking ability.

just pain
agonising pain
moaning pain
nauseating pain
overwhelming pain

This time I could not even breathe into my pain
to release it, and create space.
I could not bring my Spaciousness into the pain.
I could not turn the pain into a self-reflection,
and an investigation.

This time the pain had taken full control over my
body and my mind.
This time I had completely lost control over my
body and mind.

There, in the pain,
it was unknown territory.
The pain was in charge.

"I" did not exist anymore, for sure.
'I' was only pain.
I could not see, or feel myself
outside the pain anymore.

The degree of the pain, its intensity,
really scared me.

I knew this time,
I could not handle it on my own.

So I asked the world
for a healing circle.
You, friends, here and far, family,
help me.
Send me your love.
Carry my painful body.

During the healing circle, I felt each healing
energy sent by friends and family
like a glowing, loving candle,
burning for me.

And it dawned on me

how difficult
it had been to carry this sickness and pain
on my own
during those long months.

How lonely
my body and my heart
had been.

How heavy a toll,
I had put on them.

Oh body, oh my heart,
I am so sorry, so sorry.
Forgive me, please forgive me.

It has been so hard for you.
I am so sorry.

It is so hard for you.
I am so sorry.

Please forgive me.

~~~~

I have accumulated so much exhaustion
and so many memories of pain
in my body,

how long would it take to clear them all?

How to rebuild not only my health
and my physical energy,
but also my energetic body?

How to rebuild the integrity of my being,
of my essence?

in order to completely healed

~~~~

Being sick, I lost
my insouciance
my carefreeness

Recovering
I gain a different carefreeness —
the true one

~~~~

.
.
.
.
.

.... slowly recovering from this blow.
slowly.

Will I investigate what happened? Maybe.
Gently, slowly. No need to rush to find answers.

My body needs a break.

I went close to some deep edges, and abyss.
No need to push myself beyond the edge.

A cleansing
it was.

A learning
it is as well, certainly.

I learned that
I cannot
carry it all
on my own.

There is a limit to what my body and heart
can endure on their own.
I found this limit.
I tripped on it, so to speak.

I am aware that
keeping my sickness and pain nearly
entirely for myself was the best I could do
to handle the situation.
It was a protection, and a way to concentrate
all my strength inward.
I had no energy to deal with well-meant advice
and solicitude.
I did not want to become a victim either, which
was so tempting.
If nobody knew, I could not give myself excuses...

From now on I will share a bit more,
in order to receive the support and love I need.

I know that if I am recovering today,
it is thanks to all those loving energies
that carried me through the pain.
Thank you, thank you so much.

~~~~

Patience, little one: patience.
Recovering after so much pain, takes time.

CONVALESCENCE
Do you know this word, little one?

Now is the time to integrate it in my life -
to allow myself to be in convalescence...

Will I live one day without pain?

For more than a year,
I have been transforming
my disease into an ally,
transforming the limitations
into new possibilities,
new creations,
different ways of being.
I must keep looking at it that way.
Go further.
Transforming not only
the physical limitations,
but also my body
and my fears.

My physical limitations
My body
My fears

Not only surrender
But use them
Transform them

I must reconcile myself with my body

I must get back my personal power

How could I expect my body to be healthy,
if I don't recognise its existence
in the first place?

~~~~

A RITUAL for MY BODY

I wrote a letter of
FORGIVENESS and PROMISES
to my body.

I did a ritual for my body,
to make this letter meaningful and sacred;
to acknowledge my commitment,
and relationship to my body.

It was difficult, painful, sorrowful, tearful and
liberating to read this letter to my body,
to talk to my cells, to my pain, to the whole.

"Please, FORGIVE ME, BODY

For I have not respected you
For I have mistreated you
For I didn't want you
For I wanted you to disappear
                    to not exist

Maybe I still don't want you
Though now, I feel love and compassion for you
And I am grateful for all the dances you give me

I want to make peace with you
I want to accept you

You are beautiful, inside and outside
You have a life, Body,
Is it possible to love something I don't want?
This is how I feel about you
You have a life I shouldn't deny
You have your own presence I need to
acknowledge

Please forgive me
For I have put a lot of strain on you
mainly emotional
For I have messed up your energy
For I have not always given you the basic needs
and security
Forgive me, my body

I promise you, my body,
that I am trying all I can,
To cleanse your energy and memories

To remove that which doesn't serve you anymore
To free you
Please help me

I promise to remember as often as i can
To be gentle with you
To rest you and my mind

I promise I am breathing into you
Joy and love, laughter and compassion
Body, will you laugh with me?

I promise you to live as much as possible
In Nature, with you, for you
I will avoid all the pollutions the world pours on
us
And the pollutions my mind inflicts on you.
I want you and me to breathe clean air
In a grandiose environment

Body, don't be afraid
You are doing a great job
Even if you are killing yourself and me
When you are tired
You can lean on my soul
It is enveloping you like a bubble of love
You can rest in my Spaciousness

Body, I forgive you
For the pain you give me
For the killing cells you became
I am also responsible for it
I understand it could have been the only way
To get your message across

Body, be gentle on yourself as well
Become silent sometimes
Listen to the voice and space
Of my Higher Self, my True Self
Swim in the ocean of my inner Spaciousness
Wherein the no-gravity you can rest

My body, never forget:
I love you and I have deep compassion for you
Even when I treat you badly
We are both trying our best

You might feel lost sometimes
I do too.
You might feel lonely.
I do too.

My body, I promise you
I will find out what's going on with you
And I will cure you
If you want it to

I promise you, my body
I am taking time to rest you
a long convalescence time
To allow you to heal and cure

Dear body, maybe we still cannot
Bounce, jump, be flexible and carefree
outwardly
But let's be it
Inwardly
I found a new joyfulness in my awareness
Can you find it too?

Body,
my love,
do not be afraid

All is perfect

Body,
when you are tired of me,
tired of being this body,
tired of being trapped in this shape,
you can turn outward to the Universe,
to your own Spaciousness.

You are also Spaciousness,
not only my soul is.
You and the Universe are ONE.
There is no separation.
Your inner spaciousness and the spaciousness of
the Universe, of the Whole,
are Energy.

Body,
you can melt anytime in the energy
of the universe which is pure,
where there is no limitation of shapes,
and no pain anymore.
Oh, what endless space to run, jump, stretch,
be free!

Body, you are FREE!
I can now sense you being free,
in the Whole Spaciousness."

I THINK

MY BODY

FORGAVE

ME...

I cried and cried out of joy for my body.

My cells, my bones, my organs went quiet.
We all became a child,
including me-my mind and me-my soul.

Watching in awe at a wonderful spectacle.
The spectacle of light and breath.

Yes, I really had this feeling of being
a child together with the different parts
of my body,
a child of wonder and awe.

So much peace.

~~~~

My body became a skeleton only.
All the insides had been removed,
as if sucked out.

I became bones only, hollow bones.
No breath anymore.

                                        No life.

And I felt:
indeed, nothing lasts,
one day I will become this hollow skeleton
when I die.

So the pain doesn't last either.
Neither does the loneliness, the sorrow.

It will all pass.
All is emptiness,
just like my hollow skeleton.

Nothing is worth grasping on to,
nothing is worth stressing about.
It will all become emptiness.
Eventually it will all disintegrate.

So much peace here as well.

                    ~~~~

                    Mother of pain, lower spine,
                          you hurt me so much
                          you hurt me so much
                          you hurt me so much
                          you hurt me so much

                    ~~~~

Is it possible to

destroy oneself
in full awareness?

Induce pain,
or kill oneself,
in order to know experimentally
what it feels like:

in one's body, heart, flesh and mind,
in one's energy and emotions?

Destroy oneself
in awareness
so that in the next life,
this raw knowledge
can be used
for others?

                    ~~~~

There is no failure.
Could I imagine failure of the breath?
Failure of a river flowing?
Failure of a flower blossoming then dying?
Failure of winter following autumn?

All are natural unfolding phenomena.
Including me, including all of us.
My "failures" are nothing more than an aspect of
the endless choices i receive and make.

                    ~~~~

If I can picture my body being empty,
feel this emptiness
when I am in pain,
the pain would have nowhere
to stand on, nothing to hurt.

The pain itself would not exist anymore.

Could I make the pain disintegrate that way?

another tool to add to
my HOW-TO-HANDLE-PAIN METHOD

which includes enter the pain
go beyond it
talk to the pain
say to the pain that I love it
ask the pain what it wants and needs
bring my Spaciousness into the pain
bring my pain into my Spaciousness
breathe space in the pain
see the pain as a child

~~~~

body still dead inside.

life force hasn't returned.

Aliveness,

will you ever come back?

~~~~

I was never meant to be born
I never wanted to be born

Was I never meant to be born?
Was I meant to pass through
my mother's womb
only?

I was never meant to be born
My spirit self did not want
to be born again

I never wanted to be born

A year ago,

I was dying.

I am not anymore.

And I don't know why

Why I survived

Why I didn't die

Why I am still alive

Why ?

*I wish I had
-died-*

I will **DIE**

the day

I FULLY ACCEPT LIFE

and accept

MY ALIVENESS

Because

I will be

COMPLETE

I must set myself free.

I am getting there.

Healing is the harmony between heart and mind

I am coming back to my true nature.

To who I was all along,
and had forgotten or repressed.

I am getting there.

ahh dear screwed spinal cord, dear damaged source of life, dear misbehaving hormones, enzymes and vertebrae, dear stuck synovial fluid, dear self-poisoning digestive system Mother of pain, lower spine, you hurt me so much.

Let's celebrate...

Pain, you never go away.
I welcome you, pain. Again.

Pain,
My lonely child

Who carries you?

Do I carry the pain, or
does the pain carry me?

Sometimes this. Sometimes that.

My pain, such a lonely child
And a hungry beast devouring it all with pleasure...

Let's celebrate...

Knowing that everything ends, should be liberating instead of being frightening. Unconditional love and joy should blossom out of this realisation.

Remember dying my love, my little one, my sunshine. Remember dying, and what is essential.

Yes, let's celebrate because today I can dance
-a little-

Let's celebrate Baby Butoh!

~~~~

Little spot behind my knee
I love you
Because you are the rare pain-free area of my body today. With my hair.

I am not kidding, there were times when even my hair was hurting. That was a strange feeling!

~~~~

What kills us is not disease, or old age.
What kills us, is the ABSENCE of LOVE,
the fear of giving and receiving Love.

~~~~

My soul, my core is the vastness of quietness.
It is calm and pure energy,
and above all,
is Love.

If I am Love, then pain is also Love.
Or rather, what is manifesting into pain, whatever it is,
that is talking in the language of pain,
is first and foremost Love.

Pain, you are Love.

Oh my dear pain, you are Love.
Pain, you are truly amazing.
I bow in awe before you.

Pain, let's sing,
let's sing the song of Love.

Pain, we are Love.

~~~~

Self-healing

We don't want to believe that it is possible,
for it to happen.
We can't put it in our little mind,
in our limited human understanding.

We have been conditioned to think that way.

We can't believe in the awesomeness,
in **our** awesomeness,
in the inexplicable.

However, self-healing is possible.
Right away.
I went through it.
And still, I find it a bit difficult to share it.
To confront doubt in people.

As for enlightenment?
ah ah ha! This is no picnic.
My little mind says.
It certainly takes dedication, commitment,
surrender, will, openness,
trust, lightness.

How many of us truly dedicate oneself to
enlightenment?

We are all already enlightened, anyway.
Because our original nature is Love,
which is the Truth of everything.
We just forgot.

~~~~

I SURRENDER
Again and again

To give
To be joyful
To peel off
To cleanse and heal
To listen to
My beautiful darkness
Where treasures lie
To create

I surrender
Again and again

To what is now
To the pain and its meaning
To dance opportunities
To the absence
To new relationships
To live in Nature
To be in alignment
With my soul

And at the center
of the most sacred
and spiritual,
the chaos exists as well.

It is good to remember this.

The road to recovery.

I naively thought that the road to recovery would be easy and happy.
With the pain lessening, how could it not be?

Well, it is not that easy and happy.
It feels more like a rollercoaster.
Up and down with pain, with energy levels.

It is as if expectation and hope were laughing at me here again, reminding me that I should not go that way. That I should not expect, not hope, not cling to anything, not even to recovery and health.

Bones are more quiet though. So are the muscles. They still talk in pain; yet it is not their only language anymore.

The femoral nerve is still as painful as ever. I still want to take a knife, open that area, and see what is inside, what is so painful, what voice is there. And remove that nerve. Pull it out.

My spine hurts more than before. It is the mother of my pain- the deepest, the strongest.

My neck might break and collapse anytime. Not a fun feeling. Cracks, constant cracks in the neck. Moving carefully, turning carefully. Robot style.

After a respite, my stomach area is again more painful than the last few months. My digestive tract is a mess.

No more periods. Am I still a woman? Or just a body? A battlefield?

I am full of accumulated pain. Walking pain.
I am full of accumulated toxins. Walking toxin.
Not so pretty, eh eh.

Up and down. How to sustain equanimity and energy to keep going?

Hope and secret expectations are shattered anytime, again and again. Again, I need to sit down on the floor to wash my feet. And standing up remains a challenge. Sounds familiar?
Yes yes yes. I have been there for so long....

I find recovery, if this is what it is, more difficult than being very sick or dying.

I am tired of it.

The road to recovery is a difficult one.

Worst, I can't talk to my body anymore, it doesn't want to communicate, to share, to explain.
I live in a fog inside.
Is it because I don't need to learn anything else from the pain, for now?
Is it because my body does not care anymore, sulks like a child and follows its own way?

I keep going, thanks to reiki. Am I becoming an addict? yeah, a reiki addict.
Reiki in the morning, reiki for lunch, reiki in the afternoon, reiki for dinner, reiki while waiting for the bus, reiki in the MRT, crossing the street in reiki-mode, trying to sleep in reiki...

Despite it all, I am on the path to recovery.
Moving forward.

Last year, I asked myself:
When I am healed,
Will I be cured,
Or dead?

I ask myself the same question today.
Will I be cured?

Can I cure my digestive system?
Can I cure my spine?

I wonder. It seems to be impossible.
So many years of pain, a lifetime of pain, with my stomach.
How can I cure that?

I am on the path to recovery.

More than my body, my mind is tired now.
So tired.

I am on the path to recovery.

How can I remove all the memories of pain?
How can I extract them all from the
deepest parts of my body,
and prevent them
from running my life, my mind,
my sensations, the relationship I have
with my body??

I am on the path to recovery.

A long, much longer path than I thought.

Where I will have to unlearn the pain,
and unlearn the tightening of my body,
to keep it together.
Now, can I start to release the tensions,
without my body falling apart?
I need to learn to live lightly again, without the
foreboding feeling of collapsing.

I am on the path to recovery.

I feel worse some days,
because I am still so tired,
and want a full recovery right here and now.
Little mind talking here.

But I can walk, I can dance,
I don't spend most of my time lying in bed
anymore.

I am on the path to recovery.

I feel terrible some days,
when depression is upon me,
and i wish i had died.
They expect me to rejoice at regaining health
and at being alive.
How can i tell them that i don't?

I am on the path to recovery.

No whining here.
I have had enough, and want to scream on some
days.
But this is not a time to become a victim and
dilute my soul. It could be so comforting, but I
never wanted to go that way, and I must not fall
into this trap now either.

I feel the beating of my soul, all around my body.
My soul has a beautiful and sad song. but not sad
in the way humans understand.
My soul is running free, even if my body still
can't.
My soul is here, all powerful, and carrying me.
Light spirit, shining energy, running to where it
belongs.

I am on the path to recovery.

And

I must not forget now.
I must not forget the pain.
I must not forget dying.
I must use it.
I must shine.
I must share.

I am on the path to recovery.

I do not need a refuge anymore.
i do not need a home.
Home is inside of me.
The refuge is my soul.
Home is my heart.

Anywhere i go
I am already home.

PATIENCE

It is hard sometimes to be patient,
and wait for healing to happen.
It can be such a slow process.
I wish at times, to have a quick and definite fix,
an absolute and secured cure, but I guess it is
only a dream.

So I am left with Patience.
Better become a good friend with 'it'.

My patience is a stunning white horse...
with pink hair.
Horse Patience is lean yet very strong -it needs
to be, because it walks very slowly most of the
time — after all, it is 'Patience',
and it must carry me through the journey.
Patience has bright, intelligent and humorous
eyes, it likes to be goofy like me, to light things
up.

Here we are, the two of us, riding slowly along
an interminable path through the mountains.
A never ending scenery of desert and mountains.

One step after another, we move forward.
Very slowly.

However from time to time, when I really have
had enough -or when the call of the wind is too
strong for Patience- we take our journey
sideways. The horse suddenly takes a
perpendicular direction and runs runs runs, as
fast as it can.

It is so delicious to feel the wind and the speed,
to feel the powerful rhythm of Patience, to
watch its long pink hair flying, to be One with
the wind, the mountains, the sky, and the earth.

When we are both drunk on speed and wind, we
come back to the same endless path, and resume
our slow walk.

And I can wait now for the day,
when I will get Life back inside of me,
I can wait for the day when i will be fully alive;
I can wait for the day when I will be able to run;
I can wait for the day when my spine won't hurt;
I can wait for the day when I will be full of
energy and bouncing;
I can wait for the day when my body will not feel
crushed.

I have patience now.

A flower.

The beginning, of a flower.

The birth of a flower.

Tiny.

In her womb.

Gathering strength and beauty.

Hour after hour,

Slowly opening.

Feeling the spring sun.

Listening to birds and winds.

Drinking the nectar of Life.

Spring

Of a flower.

Slowly, inexorably

Opening, blossoming.

A promise.

I am this flower.

Here comes my spring.

Here comes Life.

Standing naked in front of you

Naked in my fears, my wonders, my doubts, my pain, my joy, my awareness, my littleness, my shame, my anger, my questions, my goofiness.

Hiding nothing.
Hiding nowhere.

Accepting the journey.

Standing naked in front of you.
The different parts of me.
Standing naked in front of my self.

Wishing at times to be smarter, more spiritual and profound, more equanimous, wiser.
To understand better, to surrender more.

But here I am.

Standing naked
in front of
myself.
Standing naked
in front of you.

Every thing is precious
And none of it matters

i wake up from the dream of life
I remember
i remember who i am
i am awake now

i can die, i can live
it is all the same
i can have more pain or less
it does not matter
it is all the same
it can be dark or light
it is all the same
I remember

Eventually I did not die.
And I am making peace with being alive.

The road to recovery is indeed long and seems
endless.

One day though, i felt the Life Force within starting
to shine again; after so many years of being dead
inside this miracle was an ecstatic epiphany.

Eventually my body felt less crushed.

I found reasons behind some pains, and let go of deep
memories. I remembered more.

Losing my mind, absences or epilepsies
- however these experiences are named -
happens more frequently here and then,
and takes different forms.
After the first reaction of fear and dread,
I learn to look at these episodes as a different way of
being, as a gateway to a reality much bigger than
what my mind could grasp.

I am learning to not be overwhelmed by
the sadness of the world,
but transcend it instead into Love.

A few years after having written these notes,
I moved to the countryside.
The pain goes, softens, comes back, vanishes,
whispers, shouts .
My heart weakens.

Surrounded by nature, I heal. I simply am.
All is perfect.

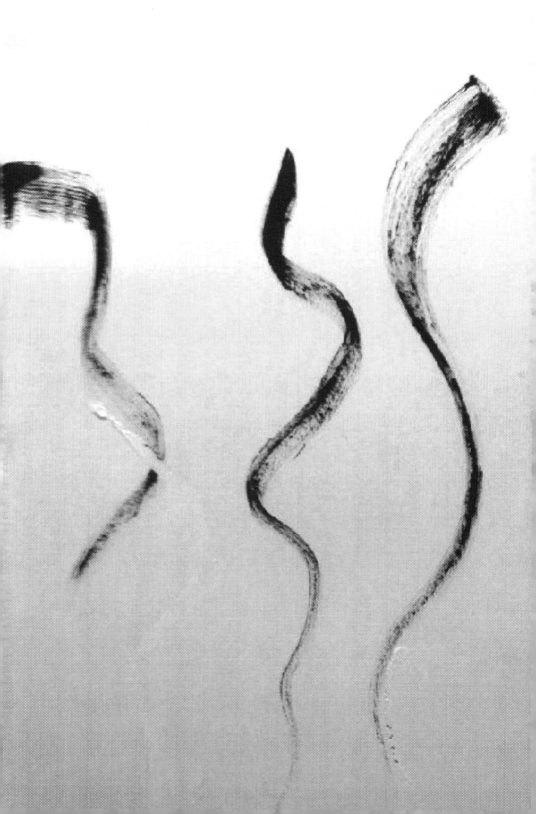

Printed in the United States
By Bookmasters